Wild Camping The Wild Atlantic Way

A tale about Ireland, cycling, and self-discovery

Will Nel-Barker

www.WillCycle.com

A WillCycle publication

www.willcycle.com

First published in the United Kingdom by WillCycle in 2024

© Will Nel-Barker 2024

Will Nel-Barker asserts the rights to be identified as the sole author of this work, in accordance with the UK's Copyright, Designs and Patents Act 1988

ISBN: 979-8-8799442-8-0

All rights reserved. No part of this work may be reproduced, stored in a retrieval system, distributed or transmitted in any form, or by any means, without the explicit prior permission of the owner.

This book is a non-fiction account of the experiences of the author, and the author states the contents are true to best of his recollection.

The author and publisher disclaim, as far as the law permits, any liability arising directly from the use, or misuse, of any information contained in this book.

"The hill is not *in* the way,
the hill *is* the way"

This started as a cycling philosophy, but to me has since become a life philosophy. Simply put, challenges make us stronger.

Recapturing an adventurous childhood

I've been cycle touring for a long time. As a young schoolboy of around 10 or 11, some friends and I would tie some blankets to our bicycles' top tube, then cycle out of town, to go camping near a reservoir some 20km outside of town.

Oh sure, 20km each way isn't far, but for a 10yo boy and his mates, it was a proper adventure, especially since there were no adults with us. We didn't have tents, and few bits of actual camping kit, but that didn't stop us. We'd have backpacks on, stuffed with water, food, and perhaps a change of clothes, and at our chosen camping spot, we'd make a camp fire.

On any camping trip, our staple food was potatoes, which we simply rolled into the fire, and oranges, which we had to cycle an extra 10km (each way) to go nick from farmers' orchards. This care-free childhood instilled in me a deep-rooted thirst for adventure, and an approach to life that makes it easier to roll with the punches.

However, as John Lennon famously sang, life is what happens while you're busy making other plans, and life did indeed happen. The boy grew up, and I went *years* without owning a bicycle.

There was around a decade or so, that I was very much into fast motorcycles, though when my eldest was born, my riding style completely changed, as I felt I shouldn't take the same risks any more.

The shotgun went off with a loud blast, and instantly we knew we were in trouble.

One of us must've set off the trip wire the farmer had set up in his orchard, precisely to guard against thieves like us. Thankfully, it wasn't set up well, and the shot whooshed harmlessly over our heads.

Two things were immediately obvious:
1) The farmer will have heard the shotgun, and will soon come and investigate, and
2) We needed to get away very quickly, and hide

We simply grabbed our backpacks, with precious few of the large, juicy and extremely sweet oranges we managed to nick, and ran for the fence.

We picked up our bicycles and carried them the two or three metres to the tarred road, so our tyre tracks in the dirt wouldn't give us away, then pedalled like fury.

Just a few kilometres away was a culvert under the road, and it was with great relief that we got off the road and hid inside it, knowing the farmer would be driving up and down, looking for likely suspects.

A group of 10yo boys would certainly get investigated, and we'd be in huge trouble, if caught.

That was an important change to my mindset, and probably laid the foundations for me later starting to favour what I call *gentle adventures.*

When my kids were old enough, I taught them to ride bikes. Living in Plymouth at the time, having moved to the UK from South Africa, soon they were allowed to cycle up and down the pavement.

They got bored of that quite quickly, and wanted to go further. Of course, that meant I had to get a bicycle, to ride with them, as I otherwise couldn't keep up with them.

Eventually, that led to my starting to cycle commute, and go on leisure rides. But something was missing. I wanted to recapture some of the sense of adventure I experienced as a kid, and that meant loading my bike up, and going cycle camping.

Contrary to what some people seem to believe, to go cycle touring doesn't mean you *have* to go cycling around the world, and as I tell people new to it, even a single overnight stay (especially if camping) is still cycle touring.

Cycling the Rhine

When my kids were still little, parenting responsibilities stopped me from having overnight cycling trips, but once they were teenagers, that changed.

My first cycle tour was simply cycling the Devon Coast To Coast route, over two days. At just shy of 100 miles, it isn't exactly far, and I did it over a weekend. And just like that, I was hooked. Again.

Several other tours followed, and I started perfecting what I call a *gentle adventure*. A gentle adventure is an adventure that allows you to escape the normality of your everyday life, even if only for a short while, without taking any great risks, or needing to visit exotic places.

A great example of a gentle adventure is cycling the Grand Union Canal, from London Paddington, to near Birmingham. Generally speaking, the worst that could happen on such a ride is falling in the canal (ask my mate Dom about that – the poor man will never live that incident down!)

A gentle adventure is just what the name suggests. It's not meant to be an extreme endurance event, nor should you be risking life and limb. It's just a way to include a healthy dosage of adventure in your busy life – no trekking barefoot across Antarctica required!

Most of my tours were quite short – just three or four days, and I started looking at bigger adventures.

I've always wanted to visit Germany, especially the part with fairy-tale castles dotted along the Rhine, and that planted the seed for an adventure:

I would cycle the Rhine from source (Andermatt, Switzerland) to sea (Hoek-van-Holland, Netherlands)!

Sadly, the realities of today's world interfered. You see, though a permanent resident in the UK, I'm a South African citizen, and therefore require a Schengen visa for Europe.

The delights of the visa system include the fact that most EU nations now outsourced applications to a few private companies.

Those companies make limited slots to *apply* for a visa available. So far, it sounds pretty reasonable, doesn't it?

Until you realise that you as an individual stand no chance whatsoever of booking a slot, as agencies scoop the slots up in bulk.

This means that, in order for me to get a Schengen visa, I have to pay the visa fee (£85), the roughly £100 to get to London to apply, the £45 agency booking fee, the £36 agency admin fee, and a further £18, to have my passport returned to me afterwards. That's £284, just to *apply* for a visa.

As far as I'm concerned, it's legalised, state-sponsored robbery! And yes, I do feel rather strongly about this.

Of course, that's not the end to it: to obtain a Schengen visa, you have to provide proof of a hotel booking, or have a letter from an EU citizen, offering you accommodation.

You also need return tickets for whichever way you wanted to travel.

Now factor in that I was essentially going to be a vagrant, who'd be cycling from Andermatt to Hoek-van-Holland, *camping* all the way, and the chances of me getting a visa was suddenly looking extremely slim! Imagine the conversation:

"But where will you be staying, sir?"
"I'll be sleeping in my tent"
"So, you're planning on making yourself homeless?"
"No, I'll be cycle touring!"
"Ah. So you'll be a homeless vagrant!"
"No – I'll be cycle touring, and staying in camp sites along the river Rhine"
"Which camp sites, and do you have reservations?"
"I don't know! It depends on how far I feel like cycling in a day, and whether the nearest campsite has space for me. The entire trip doesn't have a daily set schedule, and I'll ride a certain minimum distance per day, then play it by ear from there!"

No, that wouldn't have gone down well. As it happened, I struggled enormously just to get *an appointment* to apply for a Schengen visa.

Flight-free

The next obstacle is in a way of my own making: I refuse to fly to Andermatt. Climate change is real, and I've proudly been flight-free since 2008. That meant making alternate plans.

I looked at various options, and finally settled on this:

- Cycle into Plymouth
- Ferry to Roscoff, France

- Cycle to a mainline train station
- High speed train to Paris (bike needs to be boxed)
- Get off at Paris, unbox the bike, cycle 2 miles to the next station, rebox the bike
- High Speed Train to Switzerland – arrive too late for a train to Andermatt, so forced to pay extortionate prices for a few hours' sleep
- Train to Andermatt the following day
- Cycle furiously fast to get out of Switzerland, and once over the border, wild camp
- Cycle the rest of the Rhine at a sensible pace
- Ferry from Netherlands to the UK
- Train to London
- Train back to Plymouth
- Cycle home

It's a bloody nightmare, isn't it?

By my calculation, I would have spent a solid 20 hours travelling just to get to my first stop in Switzerland!

Yes, train services in Europe are *far* better and cheaper than in the UK, but they still leave a lot to be desired, and especially French trains have maddeningly stupid rules half the time, if travelling with a bicycle.

At this point, with my frustration levels through the roof, I said "Sod it" and cancelled my plans to cycle the Rhine.

If not the Rhine, then where?

As a South African, I am very used to practically all countries demanding a visa before they'd let me in. However, one country, quite close to the UK, is an exception: Ireland!

Yes, Ireland allows South Africans to visit for up to three months, without needing a visa. Fanbloodytastic!

As for where in Ireland to go cycling, that is something that the Universe decided for me a few years ago. How? Simple – several years ago, for my birthday, my son gave me a book called Quondam, written by John Devoy. I absolutely *loved* reading that book (and you will, too, so please do visit John's website, at **johndevoyauthor.com**, and order your copy! Oh, and do tell him that I referred you?)

So much so that I contacted John, via his web site, telling him how much I enjoyed the tale. Quondam is extremely well-written, and tells the tale of when John cycled from Ireland, to Nordkap, Norway, then down to Cape Town, South Africa. He did that during the 1980s, in a time that predated always-on communication, or digital navigation.

During our email exchanges, John invited me to stay over, should I ever find myself cycling in Ireland. As it happens, he lives near Cork (the city) in county Cork, Ireland, and Cork city also happens to be the starting point of the Wild Atlantic Way.

A plan started to take shape!

Over six months before departing, I booked some annual leave, then started planning in earnest. I picked May, as on average, in Ireland May has the lowest rainfall of all the months. For an island also known as the Emeral Isle, that was quite important.

As an experienced daily cycle commuter (pre-COVID – since lockdowns ended, I mostly work from home) I was used to cycling in the rain, but when cycle touring, I prefer to at least have a chance of dry days. People warned me to expect lots of rain, and at least one person said I'd be freezing cold in May, in Ireland.

Getting there

With the outline of a plan in my head, and book-ended by the beginning and end of my annual leave, I started looking at getting there. The obvious route was to catch a ferry from Wales to Wexford, and then a bus from Wexford to Cork city.

I confirmed with the bus company that they do indeed take full-sized bikes, but while they do, it depends on the availability of luggage space.

In short – I risked being left at the kerb-side, valid ticket in hand, if other passengers had lots of luggage. Quite obviously, that's a chance I simply couldn't take.

Again, flying is not an option I wanted to consider, regardless how quick, cheap and (comparatively) easy it would be, so that meant my travel plans were limited to ferries. I find it mind-boggling that such a highly polluting form of travel as flying is far cheaper than taking the train, and a ferry!

My preferred option would've been a ferry from Plymouth, UK, to Roscoff, France, then another ferry from Roscoff to Cork, Ireland. That option made the most sense, except for one detail: the ferry-port in Roscoff doesn't have an "international area", like what you find in airports.

That meant I'd actually have to enter France, even if only for an hour, between ferries, and for that I'd need a bloomin Schengen visa again!

Finally, after looking at train and ferry times (they don't align!) I booked train tickets from Plymouth, to Holyhead, Wales (via Birmingham) a ferry from Holyhead to Dublin, and a train ticket from Dublin to Cork city. I also booked the return leg: a train from Galway to Dublin, a ferry from Dublin to Holyhead, and a train from Holyhead back to Plymouth.

Wonderful, and entirely misplaced peace of mind followed.

Trains nightmare

However, the UK was experiencing train strikes, and shortly before the day of my outbound travel, my train was cancelled. That meant I had to travel one day earlier, and thankfully work was kind enough to let me take half a day off.

The train was surprisingly empty, but the journey was eventful: at Dawlish, we were delayed while police rescued some poor person who was on the railway line. That left us stuck behind a far slower regional train, meaning we were running badly late, and getting later by the minute.

Just past Bristol, in the middle of nowhere, the train broke down. While stopped, we watched the driver walk past to the rear of the train, with a toolbox in hand, and some 30 minutes later he'd managed to fix the train.

Of course, that train only got me to Birmingham, UK, where I had to spend the night in a hotel, before travelling onwards the following day (Welsh trains were unaffected by the strike).

In Birmingham I spent the night catching up with my mate Dom (yes, him of Taking A Dunk In The Grand Union Canal fame) as well as David – another cyclist I knew from Twitter. The following morning, the pair of them met me at my hotel, and cycled me back to the train station.

The train from Birmingham was busy from the start. Not being remotely interested in horse racing, I had no idea that the Chester Races were on the same day, and while I had a valid ticket (including a bicycle reservation) I couldn't sit down at all.

The train from Birmingham to Chester was the most crowded train I'd *ever* had the misfortune of being on, and I've been on some very overcrowded trains! I was very glad when we finally stopped at Chester, and all the people in their terribly posh outfits left the train.

The rest of the journey was uneventful, and I was excited to wheel my bike off the train at Holyhead. The station adjoins the ferry port's departure lounge, and I arrived with time to spare. This was meant to be a cycling adventure, but up to that point, it had mostly been a railway misadventure!

My first ever sea journey

I'm a landlubber, having grown up very far from the sea. In fact, I was 19 when I first set foot on a beach. I've taken the Kingsand-Cawsand ferry from Plymouth before, but that doesn't go close to open sea. As a result, I was excited about the ferry trip ahead.

Not knowing anything about the ferry in advance, and having heard stories of passengers sitting on the floor for hours, on crowded ferries, I paid an extra £10 to have a posh seat in the VIP lounge. Best. Decision. Ever!

First though, I had to check my luggage in. My bike counted as luggage. Up to that stage I was concerned about the security of my bike on the ferry, as I was under the mistaken impression I'd cycle onto the ferry and leave it on the car deck, unsupervised.

It turns out that my bike would be loaded with the luggage, and that I'd only see it again in Dublin again. Of course, first I had to strip absolutely everything off the bike, so it could go through the security scanners. After that, I strapped everything back on the bike, then wheeled it over to luggage check-in.

Apparently, border officials in the UK are extremely concerned about British terrorists and/or criminals smuggling all sorts of illegal things into Ireland. Crossing from Ireland into the UK is a different matter though.

Once my luggage was checked in, I waited for the buses that takes foot passengers onto the ferry. It wasn't very much longer before all foot passengers got onto the bus, and a few minutes later, we got off the bus, after it drove us onto the ferry.

Gagging for a coffee, I wasn't impressed by the prices on board the ferry. However, in the VIP lounge there's a free bean-to-cup coffee machine that churns out a reasonable coffee, and you could have as many as you wanted.

By paying the extra £10 for the VIP lounge, I saved myself money, based on the number of coffees I drank. I don't think they factored in people with a coffee habit like mine.

The sea journey was – dare I say it – boring, with the notable exception of a very loud-voiced American lady, with a grating accent, who seemingly lives life on the assumption that everyone within a two-mile radius simply *must* hear everything she has to say.

After the initial excitement, watching the nose of the ferry close, and setting off, there was nothing to look at but a perfectly flat and calm Irish sea, and the clear blue sky above. Fortunately, and despite the American lady's voice, I managed to catch up on some sleep during the crossing.

The VIP lounge has *huge* windows, and at first I nabbed a seat right in front, by the windows. However, I soon realised the error of that, when I started roasting in the direct sunlight, and beat a hasty retreat to a more shady chair!

I travelled with Stena Lines, but there are other ferry lines. As I didn't travel with any of them, I won't comment on those.

I'm not affiliated with Stena Lines, nor are they even aware I'm writing this. However, if I had to make the same journey again, I'd make a point of using them again.

My bike was is the same condition when I received it back as when I booked it in, and the same is true for my luggage. The staff were amazing, and the ferries were clean, and very good.

I would advise you book a seat in the Hygge VIP lounge, as the extra £10 that cost me was well worth it.

My *only* criticism is quite petty: I would have loved to cycle straight onto the ferry, and straight off it again, but that really is no big deal.

Just so you know, as a cyclist, you will check in your bike and luggage, then wait with foot passengers, to be taken aboard the ferry by bus.

When getting off the ferry, you have to wait for all the cars to leave the ferry first, before there's space for the bus to drive onto the ferry and collect you.

Dublin!

I watched the Irish coast gradually turn from a smudge on the horizon, to actual buildings in Dublin. Before long, we moored up, and foot passengers boarded a bus again, taking us to the terminal. I saw a Gardi (Irish police) and proceeded to show my passport. After all, I was crossing international borders, right?

He looked serious, but also perplexed, then firmly told me to go through a certain set of doors. All the other passengers were going a different way, so I expected a bit of a grilling. Honestly, if you travel on a UK, EU or US passport, these experiences would be vastly different for you, but are common to us Saffers.

Once through the doors, I saw a lady in ferry company uniform, and asked where I should go next. Still expecting a grilling, she smiled and walked me the five steps to a different set of doors. Once through those, I was immediately re-united with my trusty steed, and my luggage. In fact, my bike, with panniers and all, was just on the other side of the doors she guided me through. In no time at all, I was wheeling my bike outside, into the glorious Irish sunshine.

I Bike Dublin

I was given a proper VIP welcome in Dublin! Several cyclists from the I Bike Dublin group cycled to the ferry port just to escort me. That all started due to a Twitter conversation.

Originally, I was planning on catching a train to Cork that same evening, but that will have left me with an extremely tight timescale to cycle from the ferry to the train station, to make the last train to Cork.

Given that I didn't know the city, and had no idea how long it'd take to get off the ferry, it seemed like quite a gamble to take.

I therefore decided to overnight in Dublin, removing any mad rush. That meant I had time on my hands, and I was in the company of some genuinely nice people. In Dublin!

I tried using Warmshowers – a web site for people who cycle tour – to get somewhere to sleep overnight, but none of the hosts responded to me at all.

This meant I had no idea where I was going to sleep, but I wasn't fazed by that. Before setting off, I accepted I may have to cycle out of the city, to find somewhere to wild camp for the night. But first I had important business to see to: having beers with the I Bike Dublin crowd!

Having grown up in South Africa during the Apartheid years, I was grateful, as well as fascinated, when one of the I Bike Dublin crowd took the time to take me to two brass plaques set into the pavement.

These plaques commemorated the Dunn Street Stores strike, which were instrumental in causing an Ireland-wide boycott of South African produce. Such boycotts undoubtedly helped hasten the demise of Apartheid.

The plan in my head was straightforward: after a few beers, I'd return to my bike, then cycle off to find somewhere to pitch my tent. The Dubliners, however, had other ideas, and kept feeding me Guinness. A few beers became a lot of beers, and soon it was quite late.

It was then that Peter, one of the Dubliners, revealed he'd arranged a room for me in an extremely nice hotel, the Academy Plaza. Free of charge, and with breakfast included the next morning! I was gobsmacked!

The hotel more than lived up to its star-rating. The room was perfect, the shower was powerful, the bed comfortable. The breakfast was delicious, too. In fact, the only negative thing was my hangover in the morning!

After breakfast, I loaded my bike and cycled to Heuston station, where I boarded my train to Cork city, literally with just seconds to spare. The train seriously impressed me, with ample space dedicated to bicycles. Apparently, they even accept cargo bikes.

After having been impressed by the train's provision for bicycles, I found an empty seat in the next carriage, and marvelled at how much better the Irish train was to those in the UK.

Until a lady came round to check tickets, and asked how I would like to pay for upgrading to first class! She was genuinely lovely though, as I sheepishly made my way to normal class.

Cork city

I was met off the train by a delightful Irish lady called Suzi. On WillCycle.com, Suzi was the first woman about whom I published a SheCycles article. In case you didn't know, SheCycles is a series of articles that aim to highlight a broad range of women who cycle.

Suzi rides her ebike, Gerti, all over the hills of her native county Cork. Despite living somewhere outside Cork city, she cycled to meet me at the station, and we went to a café opposite the train station, to have some orange juice (it was unseasonably hot).

Suzi told me a bit about Cork city, and asked about my route plans. When I told her, she made a point of telling me to stop at a fish & chips van in Kinsale, and she was raving about their food.

We said our goodbyes, as I had to cycle to go meet up with the Bicycle Republic people, who were doing a bike-bop. A bike-bop is much like a critical mass ride, but with music, and again I was amazed by how different the Irish were, compared to the British.

The man leading the bike-bop, Tom, was riding a cargo bike, carrying a PA system through which he was blasting music. Drivers in Cork city were very patient and accommodating, and allowed us through as a group without fail. People walking on the pavement would clap and dance to the music, cheering us on as we cycled by.

Ireland shares a very conflicted history with the UK. One thing that struck me as I started preparing for this adventure was how little the average Brit (at least the ones I know) knew about Ireland.

If you speak to any Brit, they'll tell you about the "Irish Famine", and would likely shake their heads in sympathy at all those poor Irish people who starved to death, due to this "natural disaster".

Of course, that's utter tosh. While there was a Europe-wide potato blight, it didn't *cause* the famine in Ireland (though undoubtedly, it contributed). Even at the height of the famine, Ireland remained a net exporter of food.

However, the food being exported – mostly grain – was a commercial crop, and the British masters of Ireland refused to allow the Irish people to have that as food.

Even worse, the head of the Ottoman Empire was so moved by the famine in Ireland that he sent three ships laden with food, to help the Irish people. Only, the food was never delivered, as the British prevented the ships from docking.

As a result, the famine was effectively orchestrated, and caused millions to die of starvation.

Today's Ireland is a modern country with a booming economy, and the people I spoke to don't seem to bear any grudges against the British, but with the clear understanding that the Brits need to stay out of Ireland's business. The days Ireland "belonged" to Britain are long gone.

I was put in touch with Bicycle Republic by the I Bike Dublin crowd – seems in Ireland cycling groups are quite supportive of one another (though seemingly with the exception of Galway).

After the Cork bike-bop finished, I said my goodbyes, aware that it was already very late in the day (it had gone 4pm) to set off riding.

The plan was always for a fairly short first day, find a spot to pitch my tent, then cycle to John Devoy's farm, near Clonakilty, the following day.

The adventure begins (properly)

The route out of Cork city wasn't particularly busy at first, and was following minor roads, though it was hilly. Soon enough I joined the main road, and cycled past my first official Wild Atlantic Way marker, on my way to Kinsale.

The road at that stage was fast and busy (it was the main road) but I had a lovely wide hard shoulder to cycle on. Well, I had that for a while.

Not far from Kinsale, on the steepest part of the climb, the hard shoulder suddenly stopped, and I was forced to ride on the main carriageway.

My biggest concern of the entire trip was my fitness level, which wasn't anywhere near where I needed it to be. As a result, I knew the first few days at least I'd be suffering.

Not overly long before the ride, I had COVID, and after recovering, just as I started riding again, I had a serious bike crash.

I don't know exactly what happened during that crash. My last memory was of braking on a downhill, on a narrow rural lane, to allow a white car coming up the lane to pass.

My next memory was of waking up, lying on my back on that lane, with four people standing over me, asking if I was OK. I wasn't: I broke my left collarbone into three pieces, broke four ribs, and was knocked unconscious. My helmet was ruined, and my bike's front wheel was utterly destroyed.

Going purely from the damage to the front wheel, if forced to guess at the cause, I'd say perhaps the white car (which wasn't the car that had stopped for me) accidentally flicked a stick up as it passed me, and that then wedged in the spokes. However, as I have a gap in my memory, I really cannot say for sure what happened.

What I do know is that my bike cartwheeled, and probably landed with the rack taking the brunt of the impact. That was evident from the damage to the rack, and that it needed re-positioning later.

It also was something that would later cause me quite a problem later on my Wild Atlantic Way ride.

On the last climb before Kinsale, I'd pull over regularly, both to let traffic behind me pass, and to give my legs a rest.

Still, it wasn't long before I descended to the harbour. I was famished by then, and cycled up and down, looking for the fish & chip van Suzi told me about back in Cork city.

Finding no such van, I figured I must've mis-heard, or misremembered, as there was a fish & chip shop. I queued up and placed my order, then went to sit on the harbour wall to scoff my meal.

I wondered at the time why Suzi would rave about the food, as it was decidedly average.

Feeling refreshed, I set off again, knowing I'd need to leave Kinsale before I'd find somewhere to pitch my tent for the night.

The famous Kinsale fish & chips van

As you leave Kinsale, there's a long, low bridge, and right before the bridge I found Suzi's highly recommended fish & chip van.

Of course, by then I had a full tummy, so had to forego what should have been a far better meal. You live and you learn.

Just a few miles out of Kinsale, I spotted a farmer's field that looked like a good spot to camp, and wheeled my bike through. My tent has a low profile, and in addition I use a lightweight camo net over the top. As a result, I tend to be quite stealthy when wild camping.

However, someone saw me wheeling my bike into the field, and that made me quite uncomfortable.

Out of direct sight from the road, or any houses in the area, I quickly pitched my tent, just as it started drizzling. All of the past two days I had fantastic weather - warm with mainly clear blue skies - and I guessed it was only fair that I had some rain, too.

Lying in my tent, I heard a lawnmower of some sort start up. At times, it came closer to me, then the sound receded again.

I was worried the landowner might come right up to my tent, and that I'd be sent packing, but fortunately that didn't happen, and eventually the mower stopped.

My camping spot was memorable for several reasons: it was perfectly flat (county Cork is hilly!) secluded enough, but mostly because it was very close to the loudest pair of donkeys I ever heard.

All night long the pair were serenading me, and anyone else within earshot.

When it comes to sleep, I have long said I can sleep almost anywhere, and that as long as I'm not too wet, not too cold, and believe nobody would steal my shoes, I can happily fall asleep.

Apparently, I need to update that saying, to include "as long as the world's loudest donkeys aren't serenading me".

Ireland is a cycle tourer's dream! Aside from absolute emergency rations, which you should always carry, the island is full of places where you can get good, fresh food, for not a lot.

Pretty much all petrol stations have coffee machines (and none of the Costa brown dishwater so prevalent in the UK) and a deli counter.

The most common brand of coffee machine is called Insomnia, which I thought was a perfect name for a coffee brand. Typically, next to the coffee machine there's a milk dispenser too.
I usually take oat milk, but as expected, that's not an option with those machines.

Most such delis have fresh food, including soup.
The supermarkets are something different again. In the UK, the poshest supermarket chain is Waitrose, and Waitrose looks rather dull and downmarket when compared to the average Super Valu in Ireland.

The range of products is *so* much bigger, and they always stock beer from smaller, local breweries.

At the time, UK consumers were accustomed to seeing empty shelves in supermarkets, with the media blaming "failed crops in Europe" and more. Oddly enough, those crop failures didn't impact Irish supermarkets at all, and their shelves were fully stocked.

The following morning the drizzle had stopped, but started again as I set off riding. In almost no time, the drizzle turned to rain, then to quite heavy rain. I was rather grateful to find a petrol station in the middle of nowhere, to grab some food, and crucially, coffee.

Gear trouble

Not long after setting off again, the road turned steeply uphill, and I started struggling to shift gears on the rear. In a very hilly part of the world, that's not what you want! I was suffering.

To compound matters, I need reading glasses, and with the heavy rain I simply couldn't see what the matter was – with or without glasses. In the end I cable-tied a fist-sized rock between the gear cable and my bike's chainstay.

That had the effect of moving the derailleur over enough so I was 2 gears away from my easiest gear. I was slow, but at least I could labour up hills again.

I struggled on like that to Timoleague. As I got there, the rain stopped quite suddenly. The petrol station at Timoleague offered hot food, which I sorely needed after all that morning's rain.

After food, I had a detailed look at my bike, and discovered it was the shifter that was causing the issue.

This early on into the ride, that presented a huge problem, as I still had a long old way to go, with many big climbs. In fact, I had mountains to cross! I needed gears for that.

It also meant there was no way I'd be on time for meeting up with John, so I emailed him to let him know. My plan was to cycle till dark, camp overnight, then try and find the nearest bike shop the next day.

John however had other plans. He asked where I was, and when I told him, he said I should stay put, and that he was on his way to collect me. That left me time to sit on a picnic bench in the sun, drying out and warming up, with a coffee in hand.

An aspect of cycle touring that is very often overlooked is being prepared for when things go wrong.

Real life is nothing like those heavily-filtered Instagram pics you see. Yes, you will have amazing experiences, but equally you will have unpleasant ones. Knowing this from the outset will mentally help you be better prepared for when things go wrong.

When you're solo touring, you won't have anyone on hand to cheer you up, and give you a pep talk. You need to be able to that for yourself.

In addition, when solo touring in a foreign country, your plans *must* at least consider what your options were if disaster struck. How would you get home if – for whatever reason – you cannot cycle anymore?

> I had travel insurance, to cover me for eventualities that I might not be able to deal with myself, and I rather strongly urge you to get comprehensive travel insurance.

Says the raven, Nevermore

I dug out my emergency supply of peanuts, and that attracted the attention of a whole collection of crows and Jack Daws. I was surprised by the large groups of corvids I saw throughout the ride through south-west Ireland. In the UK, these would have been seagulls instead.

Corvids (I don't really care which ones, though I love magpies the most) are probably my favourite birds, and I had fun feeding them peanuts. Soon some of them were bold enough to use my bike as a perch, and a few even ate peanuts from my hand.

It was at that moment, with three crows sat on my bike, that I finally decided to name my bike (which for seven years has been without a name). That day it was christened Raven, obviously after Edgar Alan Poe's famous poem. If you've never read The Raven, please go remedy that now?

Not much later, John arrived. We loaded my bike and panniers into his car, and then he drove around, giving me a tour of the local area. John is clearly very proud of the local area, and rightly so – from stunning vistas that opened up between green rolling hills, to seascapes that simply take your breath away, it is a spectacularly beautiful part of the world.

Afterwards, we dropped my bike off at his home. As it was the weekend, he told me the local bike shops were all closed and that we'll have to wait for Monday.

Sauna on the beach

Next, John, and his wife Sarah, gave me surprise: they took me to Red Strand beach, where there's a mobile sauna right on the edge of the beach! They told me that these were quite popular, and increasingly common, along Irish beaches.

Basically, it's a large trailer, on which there's a wooden sauna. Heat is provided through a wood-burning stove, which is fed from the outside. Inside was sweltering hot, and people would stay in the sauna for a while, then go for a dip in the sea, before returning to the sauna.

John also told me of a different setup, where there are old whiskey barrels set up on a beach. These are filled with sea water that was heated with a wood-burning stove, and you could pay to sit inside one. The man operating it then puts seaweed on top of the water, to help keep the heat from escaping. Apparently, that's quite popular in mid-winter.

I spent a delightful evening with John and Sarah. We discussed John's amazing book, which I still rate as joint-best, along with Dervla Murphy's Full Tilt, as well as the sequel to his book, which John was working on.

Monday morning John took me and my bike to the Bike Circus, in Clonakilty. It's a not-for-profit cooperative, started by a retired judge from the USA. One of the guys set to work on my bike, and after quite a struggle, managed to get the shifter (mostly) working again. Instead of the full 9 gears at the back, I was reduced to just five, but I had working gears again.

I could've replaced the shifters completely, as a different bike shop had a set available for just over €100, but that would have blown too large a hole in the limited budget I had for the trip. Just five gears on the back (the easiest five) would have to do.

John took me to meet the owner of the other shop, a man called Murph. Murph's a rather old man, well past retirement age, I'd say, and when we met him, he was clearly unwell. Having not long recovered from COVID, I had no intention of getting re-infected again, so kept my distance from him (he may, or may not have had COVID).

Murph seemed to be able to operate at only one speed: fast forward. That included the way he talked, and combined with his very thick accent, I mostly couldn't understand a word of what he was saying!

County Cork was instrumental in the war the Irish fought to gain their independence, and John told me a great deal about it.

He made a point of taking me to a statue in honour Michael Collins. Collins was the first head of state of the provisional Irish government that took over when the British withdrew.

Born in county Cork, near Roscarberry, he remains an iconic figure to Irish people, especially those in South West Ireland. Collins attended school in Clonakilty, and is particularly revered in the town.

Collins' provisional government signed a treaty with the British, guaranteeing independence for most of Ireland. However, the British insisted on keeping hold of the six counties forming what today is called Northern Ireland.

When he signed that treaty, Collins said "I may have signed my actual death warrant".

Sadly, his words were prophetic. Effectively, Prime Minister Lloyd George told the Irish contingent to either sign the treaty, or face an immediate and terrible war, and left Collins no real alternative.

However, that was not seen as so by many who fought for a free and independent Irish Republic. This directly led to the Irish Civil War, and on the 22nd of August 1922, Collins was killed during an ambush in county Cork.

When cycling along blissful rural lanes in Cork today, it's hard to imagine that just a century ago, these same lanes were the scenes of a bitter civil war.

John took me for coffee at a café in Clonakilty, explaining that he escaped to the café to write most of his book Quondam. By the time we returned to his home it was mid-afternoon, and he suggested I stay over one more night.

I took my bike for a little 10-mile test ride, and though unladen, I was happy enough with the gears, and knew I'd be able to continue.

Off properly, with no schedule

With fondness, I said goodbye to John and Sarah the next morning. They are both extremely lovely people, and my life's better for having met them. Despite this, I was itching to get going, and very aware that I was already running well behind schedule.

The weather has massively improved since that sogging wet morning when my bike's shifter packed up, and I was rewarded with clear blue skies and deliciously warm days – a far cry from what some doom-sayers predicted I'd have.

I was glad to have met the I Bike Dublin bunch, and the Bicycle Republic group in Cork city. Obviously, I was delighted to have met John and Sarah Devoy.

However, up to this point, it felt like I was marching to the beat of somebody else's drum, and I relished the prospect of being completely on my own.

Nobody to meet, and (besides making it on time for my return ferry) no deadlines, either.

I'm an introvert, and many people misunderstand that to mean shy and withdrawn. The truth is introverts can easily be the life of the party. However, no matter how much introverts may enjoy socialising, we find it draining.

Extroverts gain energy from social interaction, but introverts' batteries only recharge when we're alone. I had a lot of social interaction, over a comparatively short space of time, and I relished the solitude I knew was ahead of me.

When the team leader of one of the technical teams I'm in at work asked me if I'd be cycle touring with someone else, I had to explain to him that there's simply no way I'd ever do a ride this long with someone else.

Normally, my limit for cycle touring with others is around three to four days. Remember, when cycle touring with someone, you're in their company 24/7, leaving almost no chance for solitude.

Besides, when cycle touring on your own, you're free to ride at whatever pace you feel like. You can stop when and where you want, and you can change your route on a whim.

The route I took from Clonakilty took me through the picturesque and curiously-named village of Union Hall. With hindsight, I could (and probably should) have taken the R597 through Glandore, but instead I veered further from the coast and cycled via Drom. Either route will have taken me over the Poulgorm Bridge, from which you can catch a glimpse of the Atlantic.

Union Hall has a tidal lagoon, but however pretty the village is, the reason it stuck in my memory is entirely different. I stopped at the Centra shop, to grab a coffee and a bite to eat, after having locked my bike up outside.

When I got back to my bike, my GPS unit was nowhere to be found! As I tend to always remove it from my bike, whenever I leave the bike unattended, I expected I must've left it inside the shop. However, no matter how frantically I looked, I couldn't find it anywhere. The lad behind the till told me nobody handed anything in to him, either.

Outside again, I did a thorough check, only to find the GPS unit exactly where I left it: on the windowsill of a house next to the shop! Though I felt like an idiot, I was intensely relieved.

The climb out of Union Hall was a bit of a leg burner, but I had my GPS unit on the bike, the sun was shining, and I was riding through a spectacularly beautiful landscape, so I had a big smile on my face.

The coastline here is littered with inlets, and after a lovely descent, I soon skited the edge of a large tidal pool again, by Rineen woods, but sadly, the sea wasn't in sight. Though on a signed part of the Wild Atlantic Way, the roads were deliciously quiet.

Lough Hyne is connected to the sea by a narrow inlet that floods at high tide, and apparently that inlet can be good fun to play in when the tide comes in.

However, I was on the far side of the lough, with quite a leg-burning climb ahead of me. Almost halfway up that climb, I stopped to scoff some emergency food I was carrying, and to brew a cup of coffee.

I was heading straight for the village of Baltimore, attracted by the name. I could've taken a far more direct route. By the time I reached the outskirts of the village, my legs were feeling it, and it was getting late in the day, so I turned right, away from Baltimore.

If I had the option again, I'd have instead taken the ferry from Baltimore to Cape Clear island, camped there overnight, then the next day catch the ferry to Schull (it's pronounced "skull"). That was what John Devoy suggested I do, but I was trying to minimise my costs, and the ferries weren't cheap.

More to the point, had I taken the ferries, I would also have missed out on quite an experience later on, in Ballydehob, but we'll get to that later.

Eurovelo 1 vs the Wild Atlantic Way

Though I refer to my route as the Wild Atlantic Way, of course I mostly didn't follow the official Wild Atlantic Way route. There's a simple explanation for this – parts of the route are infested with touring coaches and camper vans, in addition to other traffic. In fact, I believe that – much like Scotland's North Coast 500 - the Wild Atlantic Way was designed to attract tourists who drive everywhere. The worst of the bunch are the coach drivers, and drivers of campervans on Swiss numberplates.

Large parts of the route in county Cork followed the N71, and that *really* isn't a pleasant road to cycle on.

Some parts of my route, out of necessity, included the N71, and a cyclist was killed on that road, near Clonakilty, a few weeks after I completed my ride. Having said that, I had absolutely no trouble with any drivers at all in county Cork.

In fact, along some narrow rural road, I was slowly winding my way up a long, fairly steep hill, when a driver in a SUV came driving down the hill towards me. I pulled over to let him pass, and he stopped alongside me.

Now, as someone who has spent many years cycling in the UK, my immediate expectation when a driver slows down, or stops, is that confrontation will follow. This driver however, simply wanted to pass the time of day.

He asked where I was coming from (raised eyebrows when I said I'd cycled from Cork city) and where I was going (eyebrows trying to lift off when I said Galway) and he was genuinely interested.

He explained that I could've taken a different route, avoiding the hill I was slogging up, then wished me well on my journey. All my interactions with people in Ireland so far have been extremely positive.

Quite aside from being a very beautiful country, it is such a *friendly* nation, and I must admit by that point I'd already fallen in love with Ireland.

Some miles later, going up a thankfully short, but brutally steep hill, I encountered an old man walking down the hill. Though he only had 2 visible teeth in his mouth, he smiled broadly, and again I stopped and chatted for a while. When cycle touring in Ireland, interactions like these become *normal*. In fact, you should plan to allow time for it, so you don't come across as rude.

The night I spent in Dublin, some far-right thugs attacked a migrant community, mostly living in tents, and burnt their tents down, so anti-foreigner sentiments certainly are present in Ireland, and as is the case seemingly across the West, it appears to be growing. However, I personally never experienced any animosity that was clearly aimed at my being a foreigner.

My day continued under clear blue skies, and the route alternately visited the coast, then turned more inland. I added on many extra miles through my detour to the edge of Baltimore. Of course, Baltimore is located on the Ilen estuary, and to cross the river, I needed to head back to Skibbereen.

My route previously took me quite close to Skibbereen. Heading back there brought me alongside the river, and once I reached the bridge, I continued straight into the town.

I don't consider Skibbereen to be a particularly pretty town, nor is it in any way very cyclist-friendly, but I needed coffee and food.

Skibbereen remains a must-visit destination along the Wild Atlantic Way though, even if only for the mass-graves for victims of the famine that so decimated the local population.

Leaving Skibbereen, I soon crossed the bridge over the Ilen, turning left on the far side. Unfortunately, that put me directly on the N71, which is not a pleasant road to cycle.

In Skibbereen you will find a sombre sight. In the Abbeystrowry cemetery there are four mass burial sites, dating back to the Irish Famine.

These mass graves were once known as "the pits", and it is believed that between 8 000 to 10 000 people were buried there.

Most of the dead were effectively simply dumped, without any coffin, often in the middle of the night. There were no records kept, no graveside ceremonies, no priests attending, and no grave markers.

Over a *third* of the immediate region's population died from famine, between 1841 and 1852. The death toll reduced dramatically after 1848, but even then, there were around one hundred famine victims *per week* being buried during December 1849.

If you ever visit the area (and you really should) do pay a visit to the Abbeystrowry cemetery, and spend a few minutes to simply stand there in silence, then spare a thought, and show some respect for the many thousands of desperately poor people buried there.

It's a fast, busy and in places narrow road. Hindsight is a great thing, and if I could ride the route again, I'd follow a rural lane that runs roughly parallel to the north of the N71 for quite some distance, despite that rural road being far more hilly.

Of course, I was simply following the signed Eurovelo route, which in turn simply followed the N71, and I was rather glad when I arrived in Ballydehob.

Ballydehob

As I cycled into Ballydehob, it was late afternoon, and I decided I'll pitch my tent somewhere near the village that night. First priority was an ice-cold cider though, but as I cycled up the steep main road of the village, *all* the pubs were shut!

I was gobsmacked by this, as I was led to believe the Irish love their pubs, and that practically any village would have one, or more pubs, open most of the time.

I made it to the very top of the village (the hill continued further) then turned around and slowly started rolling downhill.

As I passed a pub called Sandboat, I spotted three young people going in, and I pulled over. They soon emerged, carrying drinks, and confirmed the pub had just opened for the day. Apparently, being still near the start of May, it wasn't proper tourist season yet, hence some pubs being slow to open.

I wasted no time getting a drink ordered (a cider, if you must know) then stood outside by my bike. Everything I experienced so far in Ireland told me my bike would be safe, but I still wasn't taking chances.

On Twitter I'm friends with a man who went cycle touring in Europe. Somewhere in Spain, on a sweltering hot day, he briefly popped into a shop, to buy a cold drink. When he left the shop, his bike, plus ALL his gear, was gone! I had no intention of that happening to me.

While standing there, I started speaking with the young people. It turned out they were two couples (one member wasn't there at the time, and only joined us later) who lived in their vans, and made a living from their YouTube channels.

The YouTubers

Isabel and Tom (LostInTransit on YouTube) are from Bodmin, in Cornwall, which is quite near to where I live, and we were all surprised by the coincidence. Philly and Keely are from Northern Ireland, and on YouTube they're ChapterByChapterVlog. As I'm writing this, Philly and Keely are currently in Australia.

After a while, we went across the road, to a different pub, called Rosie's. While speaking to them, it was soon obvious they didn't know Ireland's history well at all. I'm no expert, but I did my homework before the trip, and of course I had the benefit of John Devoy's insight.

As we were sat there, discussing Irish history, and the events leading up to Irish independence, the civil war that followed, and various other bits, I found that I was giving them quite an education.

It was then I heard a man's voice, in a strong Irish accent, say "Excuse me".

At the next table over was a very stern-looking older man, and he was looking directly at me. Next thing, he started firing questions at me. I couldn't answer all of his questions, but managed to answer most. Whether he *liked* my answers I couldn't tell.

His demeanour was possibly best described as politely hostile at that point, and it felt like I was being interrogated. At some point, he clearly decided that I'd passed whatever test he'd set for me, and his attitude towards me did a 180-degree turn.

He leaned over, and with a warm smile on his face, simply said "Thank you for understanding", then shook my hand. Next, he dragged his chair over to our table, and started buying drinks. I've no idea why, during that entire exchange, he singled me out, but it was quite an experience.

At some stage, he asked how I came to be in Ballydehob, and I told him about my cycling adventure. When he learnt that I'd be camping all the way, he directed me to an area by the old railway bridge, and assured me nobody would trouble me. He added that, if anyone questioned what I was doing there, to simply refer them to him.

Having only had a liquid supper, when I finally left the pub I decided to rather walk my bike down the hill to where I would pitch my tent, as I certainly wasn't in a fit state to ride!

Fresh soup!

The following morning was quite a late start. The YouTubers all slept in a van parked not far from where I pitched my tent, and they made me a cup of coffee. The two couples were making a video for their YouTube channels, and it was fascinating watching them go about doing so with natural ease, and surprising professionalism.

With hindsight, I shouldn't have been surprised – you don't get to live off the proceeds of your YouTube channel if you're not good at it, but they made it look so easy!

Towards the end, Tom asked me to hold the camera and video all four of them. When done, he took the camera from me, and turned it on me. Much later, I smiled when I saw they included all that in one of their YouTube videos.

Once we said our goodbyes, I grabbed breakfast at the local petrol station's deli. Spotting some bread rolls that looked like they contained cheese, I asked the old man working there if it was indeed cheese.

With a look bordering on what you'd give a misbehaving, stupid child, he told me "Those are butter rolls! To have with the soup!"

Soup?? Up to that point I hadn't realised that soup was an option, so asked for a bowl of it. The reply I received was "Well, I don't know if it's ready yet!" With that, he scooted round the counter, lifted a lid on a pot of freshly-made soup, and told me with a proud smile that it's now ready.

He filled a container with soup, and I paid for that, my bread rolls and a coffee, then went to sit at a picnic bench outside to enjoy my delicious breakfast, and soak up the sun. This was the second day of the whole trip that I started the day's cycling with a hangover!

Eventually, I mounted my bike and said goodbye to Ballydehob. It was also time to leave the Mizen (it's pronounced Mizzen, not my-zin) peninsula and start heading to the Sheepshead peninsula.

Regardless which peninsula I was on, everywhere was simply stunningly beautiful. In fact, I cannot recall any part of the Irish countryside that can be described any way other than stunningly beautiful.

British people will instantly have at least some degree of familiarity with the landscape, but though similar, it's not the same as the UK.

Sheepshead and a bee

After the previous day's riding on the N71, I didn't want to ride on a seemingly busy road, and the road to Schull certainly seemed busy. As a result, when I left Ballydehob, I followed a more rural lane, which cut across the neck of the Mizen peninsula.

Eventually, that led me back onto the R591, which circles the coast of the Mizen, but it was only for a short two miles. Once I reached the village of Durrus, it was time for some refreshments, and I was surprised to see a charity shop. Unlike the UK, where every high street seems to have several, this was the first charity shop I'd seen in Ireland.

Leaving Durrus took me on the L4704 – a road with an 80 km/h speed limit, and it was fine to cycle along. As the road skirted the Durrus estuary, I was again struck by how devastating sea level rises would be to this part of Ireland, with several roads being barely higher than the current high-tide levels.

The views along that road were simply spectacular though, with the Mizen visible just across the narrow stretch of water. Despite the views, after only three miles, I turned away from the water's edge, to seek out quieter lanes to ride on.

To be honest, the L4704 wasn't bad to ride on, and soon enough the lane I was riding along rejoined it, by Owen's Island.

The weather continued to bless me with yet more sunshine and hot days, and was starting to regret not having brought any sunscreen with me. Ordinarily, sunscreen isn't exactly at the top of your list of priorities when planning a trip to Ireland.

In fact, courtesy of my mixed-race heritage, therefore being fairly dark skinned, I normally don't bother with sunscreen at all.

Stunning as it is, my memories of the Sheepshead peninsula aren't all positive. Somewhere, on a lovely little descent, a bee or wasp hit me in the face, and stung me just below my left eye.

British horseflies seem to view me as a delicacy of some sorts, and would hunt me out in a group of people, so I tend to carry antihistamine with me when cycle touring.

I immediately pulled over, swallowed an antihistamine, and splashed some water onto my face. As luck would have it, just about a mile later there was a café, the Old Creamery, and I stopped to wash my face properly, have an ice-cream and yet more coffee, and to fill my water bottles.

I got talking with a young couple, who had two small kids. They were from Dublin, driving a hired a campervan, taking their kids along the Wild Atlantic Way. We swapped some stories, and yet again I was struck by how incredibly *friendly* the Irish were.

Not long after, we said our goodbyes, and I remounted my bike, while they returned to their campervan.

I was tempted to ride out to Sheepshead lighthouse, right at the end of the peninsula, but the signed Wild Atlantic Way route tempted me away from that.

As a result, my route from the café would pretty much go straight uphill, and I had to cross an actual mountain to get to the other side of the peninsula. When I reached the point where my bike's front wheel simply kept lifting up, I dismounted and walked my bike for a bit.

My GPS unit said the gradient was 19% along that stretch, and simply pushing my laden touring bike along took quite some effort.

It was damn hard work getting to the top, but the stunning views made it so worth it. As an added bonus, the antihistamine was working, and my eye had just very slight swelling.

That bit of road is part of the signed Wild Atlantic Way, and I found myself wondering how many campervan drivers burnt out the clutch trying get to the top!

The cover photo for this book was taken at the top, looking towards the Beare peninsula.

Having suffered on the climb, I was rewarded with some exhilarating descents. The road was quite narrow, and soon more or less levelled out. I was cycling along the northern shore of the Sheepshead peninsula, and across Bantry bay I could see the Beare peninsula.

Bantry

Near where the two peninsulas meet is the town of Bantry, where I was heading. It was late afternoon when I made it to the town, and foremost on my mind was getting some food.

John Devoy told me about Bantry, with obvious fondness, and when I reached the town, I immediately recognised the statue he described to me, back in Clonakilty. As it transpired, I ended up not sharing John's fondness for the town.

You will recall how I raved about Ireland being cycle touring paradise, and how easy it was to get food – well, Bantry was the exception.

I walked into a shop selling pizzas at 16h15. Their sign said their closing time was 17h00, so it's not as if I walked in moments before closing.

However, when ordering a pizza, I was met with an audible sigh, and the girl serving me literally rolled her eyes. When I tried ordering a coffee, I was told both pizza and coffee *had* to be take-away options, and that they only had small paper cups.

When I asked if I could sit at one of their outside tables, more sighing followed. I grabbed my pizza and coffee, and as I sat down, the girl came out to start packing away all the other tables and chairs, while glaring sideways at me.

After rushing my food, I was glad to leave. There was a pub a bit further down, and I picked that pub for two reasons: they had cycle stands conveniently located right outside the door, and they had a sign saying "Free WiFi".

As I wanted to use their WiFi, I locked my bike to one of the stands, and went in to order a beer. Well, it'd be rude to use the WiFi and not order a drink, wouldn't it?

While inside that pub, the only person who spoke to me was the barman, to take my order. As I was sat down, checking Google maps for somewhere to camp, a group of other cyclists came walking in. They were wearing matching cycling jerseys for some Irish cycling club, and looked me up and down, before ignoring me.

As I said before, I'm an introvert. That doesn't mean I'm a shy wallflower. It means that my batteries only recharge when I'm on my own. I really enjoy socialising, but socialising also drains my energy. As a result, I'm perfectly happy if people want to leave me alone.

Having said that, I found it odd (and still find it so) that a group of cyclists would completely blank another cyclist. In fact, when I encounter another touring cyclist, I always stop to have a chat with them, and I've had other cycle tourers flag me down to do the same.

When I left the pub, some of the cyclists were standing around outside, and their laden touring bikes were occupying all the other stands.

I said hello, but they ignored me, as in they looked at me, didn't say a word, then looked away and continued as if I was wasn't there.

One of their bikes had a full-sized BBQ grill strapped on, which isn't exactly standard cycle touring kit, and I commented that I'd never seen that on any bicycle before. One of the cyclists turned to me, then said "Well you have now", before turning away from me again.

Yeah, message received: you're a bunch of rude arseholes, and for some reason or the other you decided you didn't like me. I unlocked my bike, and cycled off.

Google maps suggested there were very limited wild camping options, unless I wanted to cycle well out of town, uphill.

However, there's a little shared path along the water's edge, called Bantry Bay Loop Walk, at the far end of which I found a lovely spot to pitch my tent, and was soon fast asleep.

No cycle tourers, please!

The next morning, I retraced my steps, to pay a visit to the Super Valu supermarket. I was planning on buying some food from the café, grab a coffee, refill my water bottles and use the loos. At 09h21 (I checked) I asked a staff member when the café would be open. She brusquely told me "Not until 09h30!", pointed at the coffee machine and told me to just get coffee there and not ask so many questions.

The toilets were locked, too. Big signs proclaimed "Customers only!" but despite the fact that I *was* a customer, I couldn't find anyone willing to let me have the combination to access them.

Back at the café, which still hadn't opened, despite it being well after 09h30, I politely asked about getting my water bottles refilled, and was simply told that they wouldn't do so. In the end, I bought a bottle of water, filled 2 of the three bottles, then set off again.

I was riding on the N71 again for a while, but though busy, it was OK. On the edge of town, I stopped at a petrol station, and again asked about refilling my water bottles at the deli counter, and was told – in as many words – that if I wanted water, I'd have to buy a bottle.

I was very glad to leave Bantry behind. The town left a sour taste in my mouth, after numerous instances of various different people being bloody rude, for no reason whatsoever.

Bantry was also the start of the apparent breakdown in the friendship I had with John Devoy. John had been reading my daily blog updates, and wasn't happy with my criticism of Bantry. The thing is, I'm honest, often to the point of being blunt.

Travel tales are a snapshot in time, and two different people can have two entirely different opinions about the same place they passed through, based purely on their own personal experiences.

My experiences in Bantry were overwhelmingly negative, and that was shared between the four different establishments I visited, and various different people I encountered. I won't apologise for being honest about that, nor will I gift-wrap my experiences, to fit in with other people's expectations.

To me, Bantry was a shithole and I was glad to get away from it. However, some doubts started setting in – was Bantry actually what I could expect from Ireland from that point onwards?

Grey skies to match a grey mood

There's no doubt that I wasn't in a good mood when leaving Bantry. To add insult to injury, cycling along the N71 meant I was focusing more on the road, and not the scenery. The weather had turned grey too, matching my mood.

Having no alternative, I remained on the N71 through Balleylickey and onto the Beare peninsula. In Glengarriff, I stop at a petrol station for a coffee, and got talking to a coach driver, whose coach was parked on the main road.

He cautioned me to be careful on that road, and specifically warned me against coach drivers. Later, he would overtake me, giving me a very wide and safe pass, but there were other coach drivers who weren't as careful.

Fortunately, my route turned off the N71 just over a mile further, and I was glad to leave that nasty road behind. Sadly, there are no other realistic alternatives between Bantry and Glengarriff.

Somewhere along the R572, which I was cycling on, it started raining. I escaped the rain for a bit at Adrogole Arts, and art shop and café on the outskirts of Adrogole, for a very welcome coffee, and again at Peg's Shop, a short while later. I was rather glad when I reached Castletown-Bearhaven, and decided to wait out the rain there.

I kept wondering about what went wrong for some many different people to have treated me so rudely in Bantry, but I'm no nearer an answer now than I was back then.

Outside a pub called MacCarthy's I saw a bunch of laden bicycles, and when I walked in, I was disappointed to have found the same bunch of cyclists who'd blanked me back in Bantry. Though they were sat perhaps a metre away from me, I acted as if they weren't there.

The bar lady was really nice, and directed me to the seat I took, as I asked if I could charge up some gadgets, and there was an electric socket next to where I was sat.

I stayed a while, with both big power banks, my phone, my tablet, my camera and my helmet cam all on charge. Around two hours later, the rain subsided to a soft drizzle, and I set off again. All the way up the south coast of the peninsula I was battling a strong headwind, but despite that my legs felt good.

My bike is equipped with a hub dynamo in the front wheel, and dynamo lights. That means as soon as the wheels start rolling, I have lights.

I also have a gadget that can harvest the 6V AC power generated by the dynamo, and instead of powering the lights, convert it into stable USB.

Usually, I have one power bank on charge, while the other is used to power my phone. On a ride like this, I rely heavily on the superb RideWithGPS app on my phone, and I also use the app to live-share my location, which you can see on the Where's Will page on my site.

Obviously, continuous GPS usage hammers the battery, and

though mine's a rugged, waterproof phone, with a large-capacity battery, I still need to rely on a power bank. I set the RideWithGPS app to keep the screen switched off (the screen uses a lot of power) and only turn it on briefly, at junctions. The rest of the time, the app gives me voice instructions, so I don't need the screen on.

I have an iGPSport BSC200 GPS cycling computer as backup, and I have a (claimed) 80w, foldable solar panel to supplement my power generation needs.

This system mostly works to keep me self-sufficient for off-grid cycle touring, but I do try and make use of mains electricity whenever available.

A few miles out of Castletown-Bearhaven the rain finally stopped and I even saw some patches of sunlight. The wind however remained a strong headwind that never eased up.

I stopped at a small statue of the Virgin Mary, out in the middle of nowhere. I encountered several of these in Ireland, often in the strangest of places. Looking at the low cloud over the body of water separating me from the Sheepshead peninsula, I wondered what made someone pick that particular spot for the statue.

The Beare peninsula seemed more remote, more sparsely populated and certainly far less commercialised than either the Mizen or Sheepshead peninsulas. I continued to near the head of the peninsula before finding a spot to pitch my tent.

After having pitched the tent, I started brewing some coffee, but as soon as the water boiled, I was forced to beat a hasty retreat inside my tent, by the millions of midges that started feasting on me. My tent was going to remain firmly zipped-up all night long!

Lying in my tent, catching up on things in my digital world, I saw another message from John Devoy, saying he didn't understand why I "felt the need to connect with those other cyclists".

I was surprised by that. I wasn't trying to "connect" with them – as with other people, I was being friendly, but received undeserved rudeness in return.

In my experience, when a cycle tourer encounters another, they tend to stop and swap stories, and enquire about one another's destination, plus more. I'm quite OK if that doesn't happen, but I'm not OK with people being blatantly and obviously rude to me, for seemingly no reason at all.

As for John, he's a great guy, but I seemed to have upset him enormously. I never heard from him again.

Before my adventure started, we agreed to run a competition on my site. John compiled a bunch of questions about Ireland (I wanted to give especially Brits a reason to look beyond what they thought they knew about Ireland, and do some actual research).

At the end of the adventure, I'd pick a winner from those who answered all the questions correctly, and the prize they'd receive would be a copy of John's excellent book, Quandom.

It is a genuinely superb book, and more people deserve to have a chance to read it. The competition would ensure at least one more person would read it, and many more be made aware of it. As it happens, several people told me they bought copies of the book, including Suzi, back in Cork.

Sadly, because of the breakdown between John and me, at the end of the adventure, I had to buy a copy of his book, via his website, and list the delivery address as that of the person who won the book.

Get stoned

In the morning, as I packed up, the rain had gone. More importantly, so had the midges! I rounded the head of the Beare peninsula, near Killough, and was in good spirits. So much so that, while cycling past a field of cows, I shouted "Good morning!"

Yes, I am indeed one of those people who speak to all sorts of animals. You can imagine my shock though when the farmer apparently mending the stone wall alongside me stood up and said good morning back! I didn't realise he was there, and he gave me quite a fright, but at least he had a good laugh from it.

A mile or two later, the after-effects of the crash in which I broke my collarbone caught up with me. My trusty steed suddenly started making a noise from the rear wheel. When I pulled over, stopped, and removed all the luggage from the rack, I found it was pressing down on the rear mudguard, causing it to rub.

Only, a rear rack isn't supposed to touch the mudguard! This was only possible because one of the bolts holding the rack support to the frame had sheared off. This I believe was due to the impact the bike took when it cartwheeled through the air and landed on the rack all that time ago.

I actually had spare bolts with me. The trouble was no part of the sheared-off bolt was sticking out, and I was unable to remove it.

At this point, I grabbed some cable-ties, and tried cable-tying the rack to the frame. A short ride proved that plan wasn't going to work, and I was a *long* way from the nearest bike shop! Clearly, a better plan was needed!

That better plan came in the shape of a stone, roughly triangular in shape, and about 4cm long. See, cable-ties lack the strength to hold the rack's support in place when you have two full panniers and a tent on the rack.

However, I *could* cable-tie the stone I found to the frame, so one end rested on the QR skewer. Next, I cable-tied the rack support to the frame in such a way that the weight was resting on the stone.

Incidentally, I still have the stone, and it now serves as a paperweight on my desk.

The stone supported the weight, and the QR skewer supported the stone. All the cable-ties did was ensure everything stayed in position. It was an absolutely bodged repair, but it would have to do!

My tour changed from that point onwards, as I was seriously nervous about the bodge holding up long enough. Normally quite a resilient man, I was very annoyed by the second potentially cycle-tour-stopping bike failure.

As I continued on my way, I was struck by three things: 1) the Beare peninsula is astonishingly beautiful, 2) but also very remote, and 3) the roads were some of the bumpiest I experienced in Ireland.

That's NOT what you want when you bodged a repair to a rack loaded to near its limit!

Then, to make matters worse, the bearings in my rear wheel started making clunking noises. I was absolutely fed up with bike problems, and had to seriously consider what my options were if I couldn't cycle any further.

I stopped for breakfast at the Copper Café, which is part of the Allihies Copper Museum. Allihies is a curious village – blink and you'll miss it – but I was glad for the hot soup I had.

Tiny as it is, Allihies is important in Irish mythology, and just outside the village you can find the Children of Lir gravesite.

The children of Lir were the sons and daughters of Lir. Lir was married to Eve, daughter of King Bov the Red, head of the Tuatha de Danaan clan.

Lir and Eve were happily blessed with twins Aed and Finola, and another set of twins, Con and Fiara.

Sadly, Eve died soon after the birth of the second set of twins. Lir ended up marrying King Bov's other daughter, Eva, but Eva resented Lir's devotion to his children.
In an act of hatred, Eva took the children to Lough Darravagh, where she transformed them into swans.

Immediately overcome with remorse, she tried to undo the spell, but the best she could manage was to enable them to speak and sing. They were to remain as swans for 900 years, spent in three timeframes of 300 years in Lough Darravagh, the Sea of Moyle, and finally the Atlantic.

When the 900 years were over, the Children of Lir were summoned by the ringing of a bell by a monk living in Allihies. Upon coming ashore, they were immediately transformed back into human form, but were now ancient.
The monk baptised them, and a short while later, the Children of Lir all passed away, and were buried just outside the village, where large white boulders mark the spot to this day.

Traditionally, locals would make rounds of the boulders, and place money upon them, as an offering to the children.

In Eyeries, I stopped at a café to have lunch, and fill my water bottles, when I bumped into another cyclist cycling the Wild Atlantic Way.

His setup was rather unusual – he was cycling in jeans, and was towing a trailer. We spoke for a while about our routes, which differed a fair bit, before saying our goodbyes. He already had his lunch, while I was just about order mine. I never saw him again.

A bike shop

An Internet search told me there was a bike shop in Kenmare. From where I bodged the repair to the rack, to the bike shop was roughly 70 km. I had no real option but to keep turning the pedals.

As far as my worst-case scenario went, I knew there was a railway station in Killarney, further along from Kenmare. Between Kenmare and Killarney was Moll's Gap, which is a hefty climb on any bicycle, tough to do on a laden touring bike, and bloody nerve-wracking on a bike held together with cable-ties, and with rear-wheel bearings that were packing up. But that was another day's problem.

However, I had a long way to go before getting to Moll's Gap, and the road I was on was twisty, with plenty of at-times damned steep climbs. I have no shame in admitting that I got off and walked my bike in a few places.

At one narrow, windy and steep section, I was puffing like a steam engine as I slowly winched my way up when I heard a car approaching from behind.

When the road widened a tiny bit, I pulled over, to let the vehicle pass. Instead of passing, the driver pulled up alongside and wound the passenger window down.

Again, I was expecting a robust "Get orrff my road!" or similar, but again Ireland revealed why it's such a magical place. The driver of the smallish van smiled broadly, and asked if I was alright. I told him that I was, and he stayed a while, having a chat. He asked if I had everything I needed, and if I had enough water, before wishing me well, and driving off.

And just like that, he completely destroyed the foul mood I was in, since I started having bike problems that day. Yes, the rack was still supported by a rock held in place by cable ties, and yes, the bearings on the rear wheel were still going, but I had a big smile on my face, and I knew I was going to be alright.

Still, I had a deadline, and couldn't really linger – I had to get to the bike shop in Kenmare, before they shut. However, I found the time to leave an I Bike Dublin sticker on a signpost, and challenged the I Bike Dublin crowd to see who'd be the first of them to take a photo of it.

To the best of my knowledge, none of them have done so yet.

I started picking up the pace, and desperately hoping that the bike shop would be able to help me out. At some stage, I passed the rude bunch of touring cyclists who previously blanked me. They were sat at some benches outside a café in Ardgroom, and simply stared at me as I went by. At that stage, I couldn't care less about them, and cycled on.

Not long after, I briefly stopped to take a photo of the Welcome To Kerry sign, then crossed the county border, from Cork into Kerry.

As it was a scorching day, I stopped for a much-needed ice-cold cider at Helen's Bar, at Killmakilloge harbour. There were a large number of French motorcyclists soaking up the sun outside, and a fair few other cyclists rode past, too. It was a gorgeous day to be out on two wheels.

I was sticking to the main road now, with Wild Atlantic Way route signs everywhere, and I was heading straight for Kenmare. Near the town I overtook two cyclists on ebikes. We briefly had a chat, then said our goodbyes. Somewhere I made a navigational error, and when I got back onto the main road, I got to overtake, and chat with them again.

With relief I rolled into Kenmare, before the bike shop closed, and quickly found the bike shop. Only, it wasn't a bike shop, but a sports shop that also sold some bicycle bits. Apparently, they had a mechanic, but he was away for the weekend, and wouldn't be back till the Monday.

The older gentleman who spoke with me was in a hurry to close the shop, and he was quite rude. When I explained about the rack and the rear wheel, he said "Well, you're shit out of luck. That's your problem and you're on your own." then walked away.

Google suggested there might be a second bike shop, but when I tracked it down it was more a small warehouse, and the same rude man was locking that up, too. This time his annoyance was clear, and he said "Didn't I just tell you that you're on your own?"

Clearly, I needed a rethink of my plans. After finding a Spar with tables inside, I sat down and scoffed a load of hot food. It was Friday evening, and I needed somewhere to sleep overnight.

I actually considered staying at a camp site, but the nearest one was quite some distance back along the main road I cycled in on, and I wasn't in the mood to go back. Besides, my legs were feeling it, and were telling me they wanted a rest.

The freedom of wild camping

Google satellite view didn't really show too much in terms of nearby wild camping spots, so I slowly started cycling out of town again, back the way I came. Shortly after crossing the bridge over the Kenmare river, I spotted a sign for a footpath through some woodland. Perfect!

I had to walk my bike along there, but soon after, I pitched my tent roughly 10 metres from the path. With the camo sheet over, and no lights in the tent, I lay in my sleeping bag, hearing a surprising number of people passing by on the path. I remain convinced that none of them knew I was there at all, and I slept soundly.

When you're new to wild camping (especially in England or Wales) it's quite understandable to be nervous. After all, it's a new experience that will leave you feeling vulnerable, and as an added "horror", you'll be out in nature!

For those of you terrified of snakes, Ireland's even better for wild camping, as Ireland doesn't have any wild snakes. None at all!

Some cycle touring books include detailed stats about the rider's day – X distance, Y elevation gain, average speed of Z. I couldn't care less about that. My *only* deadline was the ferry from Dublin back to Holyhead and the rest I'd make up as I went along.

I knew I allowed enough time for a relaxed tour (well, I didn't enter a race, now did I?) Despite that, I didn't have masses of spare time to hand, and needed to make progress. Seriously annoyed with the not-a-bike-shop in Kenmare, Google told me there was an *actual* bike shop in Killarney.

The Ring of Kerry

Here's the problem: I badly wanted to cycle the Ring of Kerry, but that will have meant turning left at the top of Moll's Gap, away from Killarney. That's not something I could risk, and I needed to change my plans, heading straight into Killarney.

A quick breakfast from a deli, and I was heading out of Kenmare. As I expected, the road soon headed uphill. My legs felt fine though. Some roadies overtook me up Moll's Gap – out for their Saturday morning ride – and they all said a cheery hello. One slowed right down, and cycled with me for a while.

He lived in Kenmare, and laughed when I told him about the rude man at the not-a-bike-shop. Apparently, the guy's known to be unnecessarily short with people, and my companion said he avoids the shop as far as he can. After a while, we said our goodbyes, and he zoomed off.

I was surprised my rack bodge was still holding up just fine, but the rear wheel's bearings were making quite a racket, and I was a tad concerned about the descent to Killarney. Before that though, I was told of the awesome coffee to be had from the Avoca café at the top. Unfortunately, when I finally got there, the café was closed.

The views more than made up for any disappointment, and it's so easy to see why this part of county Kerry is so enormously popular. Besides, after a fair bit of descent, I pulled in at the curiously-named Ladies' View café, and still had my coffee. Sadly, it was decidedly below-average coffee. It's a sad day when the coffee served by a supposed barista is worse than what you get from a machine.

The road I was riding on was the N71, and was part of the Ring of Kerry. Though I set off early (I wanted to get to the bike shop as soon as possible) the road was already getting fairly busy with campervans and touring coaches. It was mid-May, and so at the very start of the tourist season, and I expect that road would be very unpleasant to cycle at the height of summer.

As it happens, I had a very close overtake along there, delivered by the driver of a car with UK registration plates. The Irish drivers all gave me plenty of space.

I also encountered something that shocked me: a single piece of litter, along the entire stretch of road, from Kenmare, to Killarney. Why was it shocking? Well, since leaving Cork city, I didn't encounter any litter at all.

Roads verges in the UK are strewn with flattened Costa paper cups, discarded MacDonald's wrappers and squished

Monster Energy cans, plus various other types of litter. It's always bugged me how people of such a beautiful land could care so little about it that they treat it like a giant rubbish bin. In Ireland, the mentality was very different, and people took their rubbish home with them.

I would've like to be able to take more time along this stretch of road, as it simply is an exquisitely beautiful landscape, but I had to concentrate on the road. It was surprisingly bumpy, and also narrow in places, given what a main road it is.

I grew up in South Africa, during the Apartheid years, in an Afrikaans family, in a mostly Afrikaans town.

At the time, the Apartheid government had tight control over TV and radio, and only "approved" Afrikaans musicians really had any chance of getting airtime. I couldn't identify with those "approved" artists, nor their music, and I thought at the time that I was pretty much alone in that.

Then a movement calling itself Voëlvry arose! (It's pronounced much like "fool-fray"). These were rebellious Afrikaner musicians, and they played music I liked, and could identify with.

Voëlvry is a play on words, and can mean either "free as a bird", or "an outlaw that any citizen could legally shoot on sight". Suddenly, I realised there were *many* Afrikaners who also rejected everything the Apartheid government stood for, and that was liberating.

After moving to the UK, I rarely get to speak Afrikaans, and I was surprised when out of the blue, on my cycling adventure, I found myself bursting into song, singing Afrikaans songs from the Voëlvry artists, like Johannes Kerkorrel.

It was very cathartic.

Killarney

The road skirts two large, stunning lakes, and soon after I entered the outskirts of Killarney. The number of horse-drawn carriages on the road (they're a tourist attraction) were very welcome, as they meant I was no longer the slowest thing on the road.

Even better, Killarney has some actual cycle lanes!

A few navigation mishaps later, I stopped outside O'Sullivan's bike shop in Killarney, and wheeled my bike inside. The shop is owned and run by David O'Sullivan. I waited until he was done serving other customers, then explained my predicament.

He took one look at my cable-tied stone repair and laughed, then said "That's because you're carrying everything, including the kitchen sink!" Next, he asked me to offload everything, and we stashed my panniers in the back of his van, which was parked right outside.

David said he could make no promises, but that he'd try his best, then told me to go walk around Killarney and grab some lunch. I was worried his shop would close at around 1pm, but he assured me they'd be open all day.

Killarney is a really nice town. More accurately, in David's words, "it's a bit touristy, but I like it". It was easy to see why he feels that way. The town was *heaving* with Gaelic football fans, as Killarney was playing against a different team.

Feeling I deserved a night of luxury, and understanding I wouldn't get my bike back very quickly, I phoned several B&Bs around the town, but due to the match, they were all fully booked.

However, Killarney has an urban campsite, and a phone call confirmed they certainly had space for me and my tent. When doing off-grid cycle touring, I clean myself using biodegradable wipes each night in my tent, as hygiene is important.

However, nothing beats a steaming hot shower, and I was glad that I had at least that to look forward to.

Killarney was also a major decision point: depending on what David would be able to do with my bike, Killarney could yet become the point at which I end my tour, to catch a train back to Dublin.

Google Maps told me I *could* walk to the campsite – the panniers I was using could convert to backpacks, but it would still be rather uncomfortable carrying all my luggage some two miles to the campsite.

At this point I was resigned to not getting my bike back until at least the following Monday. After lunch, I spent some time walking around Killarney town centre, but there's only so much walking around I could do before getting bored.

Stopping in a pub, I updated my site, WillCycle.com, then caught up on social media. After that, I headed back to the bike shop.

David was busy with another customer, and again I waited patiently until he had time to update me, and the update was simply wonderful: he'd fixed my bike!

Somehow, he managed to extract the sheared-off rack bolt, and replaced it with a brand new one. Right at the start, he mentioned that the rear wheel's bearings probably simply needed a good servicing.

As that would take time, I asked him to not do that, and to instead go for a far quicker option: just replace the wheel.

David is one of those bicycle mechanics that have an intuitive feel for what they do, and it was obvious in his work. Equally obvious was that he was a genuinely nice, friendly and kind man – you could tell from the way he dealt with his customers.

The repair bill was very reasonable, too. He *knew* I was desperate, and could easily have exploited that, but he didn't.

It was far too late to set off on my tour, after I wheeled my bike out of David's shop, retrieved all my luggage from the back of his van and loaded the bike back up, so I simply headed to the campsite.

An actual campsite

A friendly lady checked me in, and showed me where to pitch my tent. In next to no time, I was all set up. After enquiring about where the nearest Super Valu was, I opted to walk there.

When cycle touring, I usually carry a pair of trainers, for wearing when off the bike. Obviously, I ride with pedals that cleats fitted to the underside of my cycling shoes clip into, so my feet are attached to the bike. While I *can* walk in my cycling shoes, walking in trainers is more comfortable.

Besides, it'd give my feet a rest from the cycling shoes, with their very rigid soles, and give the shoes time to air out a bit.

I bought some hot food from the local Super Valu, and mainly scoffed it all while walking the mile or so back to the camp site. As I got back to my tent, some French motorcyclists were pitching their tents a few metres away. I had a great spot: tucked away in a corner.

With a full tummy, it was time for proper luxury: that steaming hot shower. Most campsites charge for showers, with a machine you have to feed with coins, and this one was no different. Pre-armed with a handful of Euro coins, I finally had a delicious shower.

GAA – Gaelic Athletic Association

Throughout Ireland, the most popular sports are Gaelic football, and hurling. All countries have central sports bodies, but the GAA is rather different.

For starters, the competitors and team members are amateurs, and that makes a huge difference – there are no professional football players being paid obscene amounts of money.

More importantly, the GAA has been very closely linked with Irish nationalism, and the fight for Ireland to be a free and independent republic. In fact, several GAA clubs, competitions and even trophies, are named after prominent nationalists and republicans.

John Devoy told me how during previous centuries, the British tried to erase Irish identity – this included punishing people for speaking the Irish language, but also suppressing unique Irish traditions, such as hurling, and Gaelic football.

As a result, the Irish embraced the GAA as a form of rebellion against British occupation and rule. That created extremely deep-rooted emotional bonds that can be seen to this day. Every town, and so many villages have decent GAA playing fields, and matches are very strongly supported.

The GAA implemented a somewhat controversial rule, Rule 42. Rule 42 effectively banned any sport deemed to be "in competition" with GAA sports from being played on GAA grounds.

In practice, this meant that the games the British were trying to introduce, football (soccer) and rugby, were banned from GAA grounds. As the GAA owned their own grounds, their rules applied.

Ireland isn't stuck in the past. It's a modern country, with good relations with its nearest neighbour, the UK.

The reasons for founding the GAA might not be directly relevant today, but the support from the Irish remains spectacular, and if you have half a chance to attend either a Gaelic football match, or a hurling match, you should grasp it with both hands.

In Ireland, the GAA isn't simply sport – it's an indelible part of the national character. If you're planning on cycle touring in Ireland, this needs to factor in your planning. On days when there's a local match being played, you will likely find no accommodation available to book.

Before my trip, several people told me that I was mad to go cycle touring in Ireland during May. They tried to tell me that I'd be bitterly cold, and that the weather would be miserable.

However, while doing research for my trip, I learned that the average Brit knew even less about Ireland than what I did, and I started off knowing next to nothing. As a result, I ignored all such advice, and instead researched average rainfall.

It turns out that May has the lowest rainfall (on average – there are no guarantees with these things) and so I picked May for my ride. I had some rain during the ride, but the vast majority of the time I was cycling under clear blue skies. In fact, I got a bit sunburnt!

A change of plans

I was extremely glad my bike was fixed again, but Killarney was never originally on my route. Instead, I was meant to have turned left at the top of Moll's Gap, heading towards the Atlantic again.

All along, I planned to have a rest day in the middle of the ride, so I figured I might as well have it at the campsite where I was.

My preference is nearly always to wild camp, and there are many reasons for that, starting with the freedom you gain. If you're cycle touring, with pre-booked accommodation, then you are immediately tied to a tight schedule.

When wild camping, you don't have that problem, and you are free to stop anywhere and find a spot to camp. Of course, except for around half of Dartmoor, wild camping (without prior permission from the landowner) is against the law in all of England and Wales. Strictly speaking, it's supposedly also against the law in Ireland, but the Irish seem far more accepting of it.

However, when wild camping, you forego the joys of a hot shower. Basic personal hygiene remains important, and I tend to rely on biodegradable wipes to clean my body at the end of each day (and sometimes, during the day). But, no matter how good the wipes may be, it's nothing like the luxury of a hot shower!

As a result, my plans all along were to have a rest day at a formal campsite, and the one I was in was more than adequate. And clearly well-run.

One of the wires to the circuitry that converts my solar panel's power to stable USB had come undone, meaning my solar panel wasn't working. When not pedalling, I rely on that to top up power banks, but the campsite people were happy for me to leave my power bank charging in their office.

They also sold me some laundry detergent, and I managed to do two washes. I didn't have enough laundry for two washes, but I needed something to wear while I washed clothes, so split my laundry into two piles.

It was rather nice to have clean, fresh-smelling clothes again. My rest day was taken up with doing laundry, charging gadgets, making lots of coffee, and updating my website, as well as idling away time on social media. In between, I had one or two small bike rides around the area, including a few trips to the Super Valu.

At some point in the afternoon, I was dozing in my tent, when I thought I heard something. As I started unzipping my tent, I heard rapid footsteps behind. By the time I got out of the tent, I couldn't see anyone, except for the French bikers a few metres away.

Later, while cycling to the Super Valu, the chain came off my bike. That was because someone had fiddled with the limiter screw on the rear derailleur. I knew it could only have been one of the French bikers, but of course, I had no way of proving anything, and didn't confront them.

Not the Dingle peninsula

The following morning, I packed up, and set off. Originally, my route would have gone around the Dingle peninsula, but with the mechanical issues I suffered, my plans changed, and I set off towards Tralee.

With hindsight, I could, and probably should have turned left, towards Castlemaine, to cycle the Dingle peninsula, but I didn't, and continued towards Tralee. It was a short day – roughly only 30 miles, but with a substantial amount of climbing.

Tralee will stick in my mind for a number of reasons. For starters, the nearer I got to the town, the more prevalent the litter along the roadside became. After having cycled for so long on litter-free roads, the change was enormous and instantly noticeable.

I found myself wondering what makes *one* town's population behave so markedly different from everyone else in counties Cork and Kerry.

Tralee has a Costa – the first one I saw in Ireland. I *really* don't rate the coffee from Costa, and find it's little better than brown dishwater, made as quickly and carelessly by someone who's had all of 5 minutes training in how to make coffee. You will frequently hear the milk scream, as it's being burnt, but that's what you get when buying coffee from a chain ultimately owned by Coca Cola.

However, I couldn't immediately find another coffee shop, and reluctantly accepted I'd have to use the Costa. My mobile phone company doesn't charge roaming data fees while cycling in Ireland, though I was limited to just 6GB of data.

With taking lots of photos (which auto-sync to the cloud) updating my website, using social media, and live-sharing my location, I was concerned about using my data allowance up too quickly, so I always tried to use free WiFi whenever I could, and Costa offers free WiFi.

Just as I got off my bike, two scrawny little idiots simply walked out in front of a car, and the driver had to do an emergency stop, to avoid hitting them.

One of the idiots stopped in front of the car, and with arms wide, shouted "What're you gonna do?"

At that moment, the rather tall, muscly passenger got out of the car (I suspect he was being dropped there, anyway). He turned to the scrawny little idiot and simply said "I see you,

Paddy. Prick!"

The two scrawny little idiots rapidly hotfooted it out of there, the big lad went into a shop, and I went into the Costa, determined not to linger too long in Tralee.

After getting back onto Raven (remember, I named my bike back in Timoleage) I hadn't pedalled far before a driver cut me up quite badly. Out of surprise, I shouted "Oi!" and was met with a torrent of abuse. Fortunately, most of the old man's abuse I couldn't understand, due to his thick accent.

I still had to grab lunch though, as I hadn't eaten since Killarney. Lunch came from The Shack, on the road out of Tralee, and I'll simply describe it as very disappointing. The café seemed quite rough, but I'll freely admit my judgement may at that point have been clouded by my other experiences in Tralee.

Still, Tralee wasn't quite done with me. Shortly after leaving the café, I was slowly cycling uphill, out of town, when I encountered another scrawny little idiot, walking on the pavement in the opposite direction.

I briefly made eye contact, and that was all it took to set him off. "What the fuck you looking at?" he screamed at me, his face contorted with rage. That set me off, too: I started laughing, and he spew forth more abuse.

His legs were probably the thickness of my arms, and I'm not exactly huge. I found it extremely funny that such an incredibly scrawny little idiot thought that, had it come to physical violence, he'd stand any chance against me, or anyone else not half as scrawny as he was.

What is it with Tralee to make the young men so deeply insecure that they feel they have to grandstand at every available opportunity?

With the amount of anti-social behaviour I witnessed in a short space of time, I wasn't surprised about all the litter in and around Tralee anymore.

While having coffee, Google maps showed me a potential camping spot in a wooded area, just outside town. However, when I got there, the place was littered with evidence of boy racers, so I left again and continued cycling.

Tralee is home to the Rose Of Tralee festival – one of Ireland's biggest and oldest festivals.

You'd imagine a town that can run a festival like that would be a nicer, more refined place, but I added it to my List Of Places Not To Bother With, knocking Bantry out of first spot in the process.

Guns!

I found a perfect camping spot quite a number of miles out of Tralee. There's an art to wild camping, and that begins with being stealthy. I always try to camp where I won't be seen. After all, if nobody knows you're there, nobody will bother you.

I *firmly* believe in the Leave No Trace principle of camping, and after I left, save for some flattened grass (which would recover in a few days anyway) there's no sign I was ever there. Naturally, that means not making fires, and not damaging anything.

I also believe in being respectful, both to the land, and the owners of the land I camp on. That sounds contradictory, given that I effectively trespass when I wild camp, so let me explain.

I *never* camp on top of crops, though I prefer fields with crops in for camping. That's because I also know the farmer won't move his very grumpy bull into that field, without knowing I'm there, at 5am. When camping in a field with crops, I only ever camp on the absolute edge, where no crops are ever planted.

I also avoid camping in fields with closed gates, whenever I can avoid it, as gates are usually used to control livestock. I *have* camped in fields with livestock before, but prefer to avoid doing that, as the farmer might get more upset.

The field I found had no gate at all, and no traces of recent human activity. I wheeled my bike down a little rural track, to find a flat spot, with thick, soft grass. The long grass would also help hide my bike from casual observers, and as a bonus, the spot wasn't directly visible from any farmhouses, or from the road. Perfect!

I brewed up a last coffee for the night, had a wee, then zipped up my tent. After updating my site, and responding to a few emails, I settled down for the night.

I never set an alarm, when cycle touring, unless there's an explicit need for it. It's far nicer to simply wake up naturally, which I tend to do quite early, anyway.

The next morning, I was rudely awoken by gunfire! It's been decades since I last was woken by gunfire, but I was instantly awake and alert.

I have no idea when hunting season for pheasants opens in Ireland, and had visions of a row of angry-faced, gun-toting Irish farmers advancing on my tent, shooting at everything.

Remember, my tent is camouflaged, and I really didn't want some trigger-happy, shotgun-toting farmer to mistake my tent for something to legitimately shoot at!

I was up like a shot, and broke camp in absolute record time. So much so that I only started brushing my teeth when I was back on the tarred lane. Despite looking around, I couldn't see any of the shooters responsible for the gunfire, though I could still hear the shots.

All packed up, and with freshly-brushed teeth, I set off pedalling. A short while later, the mystery was solved, when I cycled past the Abbeydorney Gun Club! If I knew the shooting was coming from a gun club, I would have had a FAR more relaxed start to the day!

My destination for the day was Tarbert, from where I could catch a ferry across the Shannon. Taking the ferry meant avoiding cycling a large U-shape through Limerick. Besides the saving in time, distance and effort, even John Devoy, who clearly didn't like me criticising any parts of Ireland, told me to avoid Limerick. He said you only ever go to Limerick if you have business there, otherwise you avoid the place.

I had a different childhood, compared to even most South Africans. I grew up with guns, and was firing pistols from a very young age.

That in itself is not so unusual in South Africa, but by the time I was eight or nine, I *electrically* detonated my first home-made bomb. Before then, all the bombs I made were detonated using a fuse I had to light.

I progressed to using military plastic explosives, which I used to nick from the South African army.

The first time I went wild camping without any adults around I was ten years old. Me and two other lads paddled an old rowing boat across a reservoir, some twenty km outside of town, to camp on the far side.

We had no tents, and slept in sleeping bags directly on the hard ground. In fact, I never owned a tent before 2005.

As a boy, I often used to walk into the African bush, all on my own, and many times that I camped overnight I didn't even take a sleeping bag. Instead, I slept directly on the ground.

I've grown soft since! I now use a sleeping mat, am very proud to not have touched a gun in many years, and I haven't made any bombs in over three decades! And no, I have no intention of ever touching a gun again, or even trying to make a bomb.

The part of Ireland I was now cycling through was very rural, and uncommercialised. There are benefits to that – it's not overrun by touring coaches and campervans, for example – but food stops were fewer.

I was happy to stop at the Londis in Lixnaw, where breakfast was from their deli, and coffee from a ubiquitous Insomnia Coffee machine. The owners of the shop asked me about my destination, and we talked about cycle touring for a while, before they wished me luck, and I set off again.

Listowel

Roughly following the course of the river Feale for a while, it was flat, easy cycling, and before long I was in Listowel. It seems like a pleasant little town, and I stopped at the Spar, which had an actual Insomnia Coffee café attached.

Curious what barista-made Insomnia coffee would be like, compared to their coffee machines, I went in, only to be told they had major issues, and none of their machines were working.

Fortunately, I managed to grab a coffee from a deli around the corner. Afterwards, I was pondering where to camp overnight. Listowel isn't very far from Tarbert, and I was told there really isn't much at Tarbert, so I considered simply camping somewhere in, or near Listowel.

As I was cycling, and pondering this, I saw a pub with a most unusual name: Mike the Pies. Clearly, this was the Universe telling me to stop, so that's what I did.

The barman was very friendly, and when I discussed my options with him, suggested I go camp down near the river, adding that nobody would object, or disturb me. Ireland was back to its usual very friendly self!

The pub has photos of various performers that have been there over the years, and it really is an astonishing collection, given the small size of Listowel.

Incidentally, Listowel is also one end of the Limerick-Kerry Greenway – a traffic-free shared path, built on a disused railway.

Had I known that from the start, I may well have opted for cycling through Limerick. Clearly, I hadn't done enough research before the adventure.

However, that needs to be balanced against John Devoy's advice to avoid Limerick. In fact, he said "you only ever go to Limerick if you have business in Limerick, otherwise you avoid the place"

Ireland has yet to discover the benefits of cycle tourism, and when they do, I expect it'd be a growth business.

For starters, Ireland is hauntingly beautiful, and just hilly enough to make cycling a worthwhile challenge. Routes like the Limerick-Kerry Greenway is a huge step in the right direction, and there's another Greenway from Cork city being built.

The number of Irish people who were surprised that anyone would choose to cycle the Wild Atlantic Way is very telling though.

If you cycled Land's End to John O'Groats in the UK, during summer you will encounter many other cyclists doing that same route.

The Wild Atlantic Way was different, and with the exception of two charity cyclists, and the cyclist towing a trailer, I encountered no other riders doing that route (though it's possible the rude bunch of Irish cyclists were).

Also very noticeable along the Wild Atlantic Way is the lack of cycling facilities. That ranges from lack of cycle stands, to lack of cycle lanes, and crucially, how few bike shops there were.

I also didn't encounter a single bike hire place, when there are *so* many places where cycle hire would absolutely thrive.

I didn't really have time to explore the Limerick-Kerry Greenway, which is a pity. After leaving the pub, I promptly decided to ignore the advice from the barman, purely because it would have meant far too short a day. The ride to Tarbert was entirely uneventful, more so because I avoided the main road.

Goodbye Kerry

As I rolled into Tarbert, I started looking for somewhere to pitch my tent for the night, but in the village itself seemed unlikely. As a result, I cycled to the ferry stop, and on the way back, stopped, and sat on a bench to admire the view over the Shannon estuary.

The Shannon is Ireland's longest river, and the estuary goes all the way to Limerick.

An older lady walking her dog came past, and we started talking. When she learned that I was camping, she directed me through a narrow gap in a wall, to somewhere that (going by her description) sounded like heaven.

After we said our goodbyes, I went in search of this Shangri-La she described, but I couldn't find it at all. I saw a few spots that would do at a push, but nowhere that seems anything remotely like a great, or even good camping spot.

However, I had more pressing concerns: I needed food. Now I'm someone who likes a proper greasy-spoon café, so when it comes to food, you really cannot accuse me of having very high standards.

However, the burger place in Tarbert was something special: melamine tables and benches that look like they were fitted (second-hand) in 1972, and food that really *you* should be paid to eat!

Honestly, if ever in Tarbert, go eat at the pub, and avoid the burger place across the road!

I saw two cyclists pull up and go into the pub, and at the time felt that I could do with a drink, so I followed their example. I was SO glad I did!

After ordering a cider, I sat down, and the two cyclists were joined by a third person. They started talking to me, and invited me over to their table, where I was fascinated to learn their tale.

Two of them (the youngest 67, the eldest 80) were cycling the *entire Wild Atlantic Way* as a charity fundraiser. The third guy was the brother of one of the riders, and he was driving their support van.

They were amazing people – friendly, kind, and with a superb sense of humour.

They were relying on a campervan, but that developed a mechanical fault (apparently, mechanicals aren't limited to just my bike!) and had a temporary small panel van as a support vehicle.

They were also pondering where to overnight, and decided to cross the Shannon first. I hadn't made up my mind yet, but cycled with them to the ferry. When we got there, it was just a short wait.

One of the guys said I'd find a better camping spot across the river, and I instantly made up my mind to hop on the ferry with them.

Hello Clare

The Shannon is Ireland's longest river, and also forms the border between counties Kerry and Clare, and I stood on the viewing desk, watching Kerry fade into the distance, and Clare becoming nearer.

After disembarking, we said our farewells, and I watched them cycle off. Three utterly remarkable men, who wanted to do something extraordinary, and raise money for a charity that provides counselling and support to people at risk of suicide.

My life is better for having met them.

There's a visitor centre on the Clare side of the ferry, but it was closed, which actually suited me just fine.

I waited till all the cars from the ferry left, then found a really nice spot in a garden area between the road and the river.

The grass was mowed not long before, and I was shielded from view by shrubs. In no time at all I had my tent up, and was brewing a coffee. After watching the sunset, I settled down in my tent, updated my website, then drifted off to sleep.

As expected, in the morning, the visitor centre opened, but it was a disappointment: filled with touristy tat, the coffee they served hardly deserved to be called that, and I couldn't drink it all.

I'm not joking! With horror, I watched them make me a cup of the nastiest instant coffee imaginable. As someone who carries an AeroPress Go with him when cycle touring, I can assure you that coffee is important to me. Life is *far* too short to drink bad coffee.

They also didn't do hot food! With a captured customer base on their doorstep, in the large car park, they could do far better. Ah well.

It was time to hop onto Raven and pedal off. In Cooraclare, I found a service station with a deli, and that sorted breakfast.

During breakfast, I had a curious encounter: a very lovely dog came over to say hello, and while I was fussing over the dog, a lady stopped by a petrol pump and got out of her car, then came over.

Wondering why she was walking straight to me, it soon transpired that I wasn't the aim of her focus, but rather the dog was.

She started telling it off for having gone wandering again. At some point, mid-sentence, she must've realised she hadn't even acknowledged my presence, and started profusely apologising.

She went on to explain it wasn't her dog, but her neighbour's, and while an extremely friendly dog, they were worried about it roaming around on its own.

Peat cutting

While riding through counties Cork and Kerry, I couldn't help but notice there was lots of road-works everywhere, and the roads overall were very good.

Those that weren't very good looked like they were being repaired, to be very good. County Clare was different, and very soon I realised the roads were in far worse state.

I was surprised to also spot something else: peat cutting! Peat is an incredible carbon sink, and when cut, and dried, it can be used in place of firewood.

At one point, I saw two worlds colliding: and old man was manually cutting peat, while in the distance behind him, a tractor was dragging a machine that cut peat on an industrial scale.

However, peat-burning should never be allowed, because burning peat releases enormous amounts of CO_2 into the atmosphere - CO_2 that was held captive for a very, very long time.

I was extremely surprised to find peat cutting was a common-place activity in county Clare. I was utterly gobsmacked to learn Ireland was at the time still operating a peat-fuelled power station! Thankfully, that's since shut down.

Continuing along the EuroVelo 1 route, I headed back to the Atlantic coast, and soon found myself cycling through Spanish Point.

Apparently, during the storms that destroyed the Spanish Armada, two Spanish ships were wrecked here, with significant numbers of Spanish sailors surviving.

Those sailors were executed by the British, and buried in a mass grave. In time, all traces of the mass grave vanished, but archaeologists found the site in 2015.

Spanish Point was the nearest I saw to county Clare being in any way touristy, and I stopped for a coffee, in what transpired to be a rather posh café.

Given the state I was in - covered in road dust, and undoubtedly smelling a tad fragrant - I'm surprised they let me stay!

I also found the only bit of dedicated cycling infrastructure I'd seen anywhere in Clare in the shape of one of those integrated bicycle maintenance stands.

Except, to underline how much scope there is here for cycling development, it was rusty and broken. I was interested in the pump, but suspect it last worked many years before I got there.

My day's riding ended in Milltown Malbay, quite nearby, where I found a spot to pitch my tent.

The entire Spanish Point area is beautiful, with fantastic beaches, and it was easy to see why it's quite commercialised.

Signs of the past

Ireland has a housing crisis, and throughout Cork and Kerry (and even from the train down to Cork) I could see so many building sites, where new homes were going up.

In Clare, I saw something different: lots and lots of really old, derelict homes. In fact, the scale of derelict houses in Ireland is so vast that the Irish government offers grants of up to €70 000 for people to renovate such properties.

Many of the derelict homes I saw were likely simply abandoned by Irish people who left in search of a better life in the USA.

The link between Ireland and the USA is evident in many places, such as a field of trees just outside Kinsale, Cork.

Each tree in the field has a plaque, carrying the name of one of the firemen that died when the World Trade Centre collapsed, following those awful attacks.

However, it can also be seen in the enormous collection of USA police department badges on display in Gus O'Connor's Pub, in Doolin – apparently, all donated by Irish, or their descendants, who became cops in the USA, and who originally came from the area.

More rest days

The general area also boasts the rather spectacular Cliffs of Moher, and you can expect to encounter many walkers coming off, or heading to the walking trail.

Google Maps told me there was a campsite ahead, and as I was cycling along a narrow rural lane, I crested a rise and caught sight of the Atlantic again.

The sight made a me stop, to admire the view for a bit. Just after I stopped, a huge 4x4 came driving along, then stopped next to me. The driver smiled, and told me just a little further along there was a spot where the view was much better.

He and his passenger started enquiring about my trip, and when I told them I was heading to Galway, along the coast, they warned me that the road - though very scenic - wouldn't be pleasant to cycle on.

The driver told me of a road that the name suggested it crosses a mountain, but said it wasn't very steep. He strongly suggested I take that road, and get off the main road, even if only for a while.

After that, I thanked them, and we said our goodbyes. A short while later, on the descent, I rounded a corner and the view simply took my breath away. That driver was absolutely right!

At this stage, I was ahead of schedule, so my riding days were very short. Cities are expensive to book accommodation in, and wild camping in cities, while certainly possible, is usually best avoided.

Combined with the fixed date and time for my return ferry meant I had to have another rest day. With a rest day, I do actually prefer a formal campsite, as that means I'll have access to showers, toilets, proper kitchen facilities and mains electricity.

I found a very well-kept campsite, called Nagles, right on the coast, just outside Doolin, and promptly pitched my tent.

Walking distance from the campsite was the ferry terminal for ferries to Aran islands, but at this stage I needed to be careful with my remaining budget, and the ferry was expensive.

Blissfully minding my own business, in a campsite that was still very empty (the owner told me that if I arrived just a week later, he would've had no space for me and my tiny tent) I was interrupted by a cheeky chappy, who decided to pitch his tent *right* next to mine.

In doing so, he reminded me of the many reasons I normally prefer to wild camp. Seriously, in a vast, mostly empty campsite, what kind of person chooses to pitch their tent right next to someone else's?

Showing complete disinterest didn't stop him from telling me his life story, and I heard stories that ranged from the bank that's about to close his account, as they "refused to give back his €17 000", to his camping experience on the Aran islands.

Oblivious to my rolling eyes, he then proceeded to tell me that he has a masters degree in nuclear physics (an odd qualification for someone so obviously poor at maths) before launching into full-blown conspiracy theories about

"You know, there are cars that can run on tap water, but *They* are stopping us from knowing that!"

I'd planned on a walk along the nearby Cliffs of Moher, but without breaking stride, he suggested that we could go for a walk together.

That's when I put my cycling shoes back on and bluntly told him he'd be welcome to join me on a bike ride, if he felt he could keep up, running alongside.

He packed up before I did the next morning, and I was genuinely glad to see him go, but disappointed that – though available – he clearly failed to make use of the shower facilities at the campsite.

I had no idea where he was heading, but later, as I cycled past where he was waiting at a bus stop, he startled me and the others in the bus queue, by waving and acting as if I was his long-lost brother.

I pedalled much faster, just to get away from him, but I did feel sorry for the bus passengers who would have to endure his body odour!

The Burren

John Devoy told me about the Burren, but no amount of description can equal the reality. In an incredibly short space, the landscape changed completely, and looked almost alien.

Huge swathes of exposed rock are everywhere. It is a beautiful landscape, in a very stark way, like a giant wound to the earth that never healed properly.

The Burren has National Park status, and the name is taken from the Irish An Bhoireann, meaning "rocky place". It is Europe's largest karst landscape, and is made of limestone.

With hindsight, I wished I'd camped somewhere on the Burren, instead of that campsite.

The downside is there were effectively two roads between where I was, and Galway: the R477, or the N67. Traffic alone is reason to avoid the N67, but equally importantly, the R477 is a scenic, coastal route, with far better views.

Unfortunately, that road is also quite narrow in places, and rather twisty. At one place, a dry-stone wall had partially collapsed onto the road, and a woman driving a VW Transporter in the opposite direction had stopped, and started clearing sizeable rocks from the road.

I pulled over and started helping. We were in a hurry, as it was just after a blind rise, and oncoming drivers will have been unable to see the rocks, until it was too late.

I literally cleared the last rock seconds before two cars came speeding through!

Of course, no good deed goes unpunished, and my punishment came in the shape of several large coaches giving me extremely close overtakes.

The driving along that road was by far the worst I experienced anywhere in Ireland, and by far the worst drivers were those behind the wheel of Transport for Ireland coaches! In notable second place though, are campervans with Swiss number plates.

Nearing Galway

The coastal road through the Burren was getting to me. Most of the way there simply was nowhere to get out of the way of the murderous coach drivers, and I suffered many close overtakes. The turning the 4x4 driver previously told me about couldn't come soon enough!

When I got to the turning near Abbey Hill, I was ready to tackle big climbs, if that meant avoiding the main road! However, that man was absolutely right: the steepest climb was just 6%, and the road was blissfully quiet.

It was still a scorcher of a day though, and sweat was dripping off me.

This was my last full day of cycling, and a longer day than recent days, with about 60 miles of cycling to get me to Galway.

When I first announced my plans on Twitter, a cyclist who lives in Galway offered that I could stay overnight at their home, and to meet me outside Galway, then ride in with me.

I was rather grateful, as it will have meant that I'd be able to have a proper shower, before getting the train back to Dublin.

With just a day to go, they suddenly messaged me, saying I could no longer stay over. I was disappointed, but fair enough. After all, they owed me nothing.

On the outskirts of Galway, I stopped at a café that turned out to be very expensive, but that didn't stop me from having an ice-cold orange juice. I badly needed that!

From there, I cycled into the city, to go and find the train station. My train to Dublin would leave in the morning, and after 60 hilly miles on a laden touring bike, I didn't much feel like cycling far out of the city, to try and find a place to wild camp.

As a result, on the way to the train station I was looking out for potential camping spots.

Urban wild camping

After satisfying myself that I knew where to go to catch my train, I tried my luck with a hostel, but they had no vacancy.

That meant one option only: urban wild camping.

The trouble with urban wild camping is people. Either you encounter NIMBYs (Not In My Back Yard) though of course I wasn't planning on camping in someone's actual back yard.

NIMBYs complain about anything and everything near them, and if I was spotted pitching my tent, they'd be likely to either come over and tell me to pack up, or call the Gardai (police) on me.

The next group is teenagers. I'll be quick to say not all teenagers, but there's a minority that takes great pleasure from terrorising others, and I had no intention of falling victim to them.

There are also criminals, who might try and steal my bike, or perhaps rob me. This group I wanted most to avoid!

Clearly, what was needed was some stealth camping, and I found a perfect potential spot, between a traffic-free path and the banks of Lough Atalia.

I waited till it started getting dark, then picked up and carried my laden bike through the long grass (wheeling it through would leave too distinctive a trail that someone was there).

Working quickly, and quite well-shielded by vegetation, I pitched my tent, rolled out my sleeping mat, locked my bike with all three locks, then zipped up my tent.

I was maximum 4 metres away from people using the path, and I regularly could hear passers-by talking, but nobody knew I was there.

With an alarm set for early the next morning (after all, I couldn't risk missing my train to Dublin) I went to sleep.

Dublin. Again

One thing that didn't factor in my plans was that Galway train station actually closes for the night! I was outside the locked doors early in the morning, impatiently waiting for them to open.

Once open, it wasn't long before, coffee in hand, I boarded my train to Dublin.

I also overlooked something else: Galway was playing a game of hurling against Dublin that afternoon, and lots of fans were travelling to support their team.

Honestly, the Irish absolutely *love* Celtic football, and hurling, and fans normally travel all over Ireland to support their teams.

If you plan a cycling adventure in Ireland, and have any intention of using hotels, or B&Bs, this *needs* to factor heavily in your plans.

As a result, by UK standards, the train was fairly busy, but I would never have described it as overcrowded. Irish Rail felt differently, and halfway along, passengers were offered the chance to leave the train, and take the coaches laid on especially due to the "overcrowding".

From Heuston station, it was an easy cycle to my hostel, then I had a final catch-up with the I Bike Dublin crowd.

They really are a genuinely nice bunch of people, and in a country full of genuinely nice people, to stand out due to being nice takes some doing!

Obviously, I've only had limited experience of cycling in Dublin, but I found cycling in the city to be really easy, and subjectively far safer than risking your life when cycling in Plymouth.

Homeward bound

I stayed in a hostel overnight, and while it was clean, it wasn't a pleasant experience. The fellow guests had zero consideration for anyone else, and various people came and went, at various times of the night, all talking loudly and making noise.

As a result, I had very little sleep, and eventually decided to pack up and head off to the ferry port quite early. As compensation, I had an amazing bike ride through the streets of Dublin, early the next morning. For a short while, there was a fox trotting along as it owned all of Dublin, staying in the middle of the road, while I rode in the cycle lane.

Of course, like Galway station, the ferry port also wasn't open 24/7, and I spent a good hour hanging around before they opened.

The ferry trip was unremarkable, save for one thing: nobody asked to see my passport, nor any other form of ID! Effectively, I could have crossed into the UK without a passport!

Also, unlike what was the case when I crossed from the UK to Ireland, I didn't have to put my luggage through a scanner. Obviously, it may well have been scanned after I checked my luggage in, without me knowing about it.

The ferry was simply a reverse-direction of my earlier ferry journey, and again I had plenty of coffee, and managed to fit in a snooze.

As I mentioned at the start of this tale, the ferry and train times don't align, so I had a few hours before my train from Holyhead departed. I whiled the time away by cycling around, out to the end of the breakwater.

It was a culture-shock all over again. From my recent experience of cycling in Ireland, I wasn't used to so much litter everywhere anymore, nor so many boarded up shops, betting shops and charity shops on the high street.

This may sound like I'm trying to slag off the UK, but if you did a similar journey, you will be just as shocked by the difference, once back in the UK.

When I got back to the train station, I didn't have to wait long for my train to arrive. This train I was taking followed a different route, and didn't divert via Birmingham. Instead, it crossed Wales.

I had a seat and a bike space booked, which I was grateful for, as that train rapidly filled up. Though not *quite* as packed as the train between Birmingham and Chester, we still had loads of people sitting on the floor. Again, the contrast between this, and the train from Galway to Dublin was striking.

The train from Holyhead was running late, and that was a major problem, as I had just 6 minutes for me to get off, find my connecting train home, and board it.

When we were running 15 minutes late, I asked the train manager about the connecting train. I simply didn't have enough time left to cycle from near Cardiff down to

Plymouth, and the next train would only be the following day.

The train staff were good as gold, and when conditions permitted, the driver actually sped up, and reduced our lateness. They also arranged to hold the train down to Plymouth. When we got to the station where I had to switch trains, I made it onto the other train by only a few seconds. The train to Plymouth started moving before I even had chance to start looking for a seat.

The train journey down to Plymouth was entirely uneventful, save for a bunch of rowdy teenagers who boarded at Dawlish, and who clearly had a great evening already. Peace soon descended on the train, after the party-crowd got off at the next station, and I arrived in Plymouth just after eleven at night.

Post adventure blues

I firmly believe that an adventure starts, and ends, at your front door. Do not be fooled into rushing to and from whatever your destination is – the journey is part of the adventure.

I arrived back home late at night, but had the following day off from work still. That allowed me at least some time to unpack all my stuff, do laundry, and even have a bit of a lie-in.

Though I had the opportunity to sleep in a real bed, in the hostel in Dublin, being back in my own bed was bliss.

However, over the following week, or so, as I was back at work, and the normal routine of my life returned, I found myself reliving the adventure in my head.

After any such adventure, I usually suffer from a bout of post-adventure blues. Sometimes, we experience something called Type 2 fun – activities that didn't seem fun at the time, but which we see as fun, when looking back.

It wasn't fun when my bike started developing issues, and on two occasions I thought I may have to cut my adventure short. Looking back, even those times seem like fun now.

Usually, I like to digest things for a while, before writing about them. However, during my Wild Atlantic Ride however, I had to post daily updates to my website.

I'm in a habit of taking voice notes along a ride (using a speech-to-text app on my phone) and I certainly recorded many rambling thoughts, ideas and more.

Most of that never made it onto my site, and much of it never made it into this tale. Some things are simply too personal, too precious to share.

I had to digest the adventure in my head first, before I could write about it.

Of course, I was (and probably still am) looking at Ireland through rose-tinted glasses.

My adventure was flavoured as much by the splendour of the landscape, and the gregariousness of the people, as it was by the utterly unexpected bout of warm, dry weather, and the fact that – for a while, at least – I escaped pretty much all responsibilities in my life.

Knowing that doesn't alter anything though, as Ireland remains hauntingly beautiful. When you go cycle touring in Ireland (and you really, *really* should!) I expect you too will fall in love with the country, and the people.

Future plans

I'm not done with Ireland! For starters, I'd love to go cycle the bottom half of the Wild Atlantic Way again. Next time, I'd avoid the ferry at Tarbert, and cycle through Limerick.

I'd also do a full loop of the Mizen peninsula, do the full Ring of Kerry, and cycle the Dingle peninsula.

However, before that, I'd love to go cycle the top half of the Wild Atlantic Way! Of course, that would require a large chunk of annual leave, plus probably at least £2 000 in spending money.

More importantly, I might have quite a departure from my normal routing, and beforehand see if there were any Irish cyclists who wanted to cycle small parts of the way with me.

You get to learn far more about a place when you have a local along, telling you at least some of it – that's something John Devoy demonstrated very well.

As for when any of this will happen – sadly not for quite some time, but that doesn't mean I can't start planning.

About Will

Will is a South African, permanently settled in Devon (or, as he prefers to call it, Heaven) in the UK.

An avid cyclist, Will has a web site called **www.WillCycle.com**. The site focuses on cycle camping and cycle touring, and offers arguably the best, most-detailed collection of traffic-free cycle route guides for such UK-based routes.

When not out cycling, working on his web site, or writing about cycling adventures, Will is employed as a network security engineer.

Finally, Will finds it very awkward to write about himself in the third person.